EXERCISING THE PAIN AWAY

*A cultural spin on
eating disorder and despair*

By
Veronica Foster

Published by Impression Publishing
Tel: 01487 843311
www.printandpublish.co.uk

All rights reserved.

First Edition published 2012

©.Veronica Foster 2012

Printed and bound in Great Britain
Impressions Print And Publish

A catalogue record for this book
is available from The British Library
ISBN 978-1-908374-24-0

Special Mention

To my dad who was my hero and my guide. I miss your sense of humour and your guidance.

To my mum who was my best friend and my guide. I miss your beautiful smile; you were a beautiful, kind mum – the best.

To my big brother who was my gentle giant who was always full of guidance. I miss your advice and your support.

To my lovely auntie who was so kind and did everything you could to help me and my family. I miss you so much.

To my special friend, you were a true friend to me because you were always so honest and I could trust you. I miss your energy for life and all the great times we had together – you left us too early.

This book is in memory of all of you to say that I lost some special people in my life. You will all forever live on in my heart and my thoughts – I'll never forget you. I'll never let you out of my heart. You will always be here with me. I'll hold onto the memories.

Acknowledgements

To Jackie and Natalie Bailey. Thank you for all the time you spent making sense of my writing in the first stage of this book.

To Shabina. Thank you for all your help and advice. You always put yourself out to help me.

To Lisa, my lovely niece. Thank you for the many hours, day and night, that you spent on the book. I can't thank you enough. Your old Aunty loves you.

To Anton, my wonderful nephew. Thank you for doing such a fantastic job on the cover. Love you lots.

To Tony. Thank you for all the time you spent, providing your expertise. I really appreciated it.

To Gloria. Thank you for helping me complete the book.

Chapters

Childhood
1. Introduction 3
2. My Childhood...4
3. Puberty Trouble 5
4. My Early Years Home Life 7
5. My Career...10
6. Siblings..11

Adolescent Years
7. College Life 13
8. Life After College.......................................15
9. Dad and Mum's Health...............................17
10. My First Holiday..18
11. Dad's Health..20
12. Grandad 21

My Body Shape
13. Dad's Stroke..23
14. Diet and Gym...27
15. Dad Comes Home 30
16. Dad's Relapse..32
17. Dad's Death...35
18. Saying Goodbye...36
19. Life After Dad's Death 39
20. My Diet Takes Over....................................41
21. Doing As I Am Told 45
22. Hospital Treatment.....................................48

Is This Recovery?
23. Visiting Jamaica With My Mum...................51
24. Back to Life 53
25. Day Care...54
26. Disappointment with Day Care...................56
27. New Treatment Therapist 58
28. Hospital Admission....................................61
29. Home Again...64

Thoughts and Emotions
30. Mum's Relapse 68
31. Mum's Discharge 70
32. My Diary Entries..................................71
33. Diary Entries 2003 78
34. Nursing Home......................................85
35. My Brother 86
36. Losing Someone Special 90
37. Trying To Cope Again 93

Am I Taking Control Or Is The Exercise Controlling Me?
38. Running...96
39. My Health Problems 98
40. Trying To Take Control Of My Life 100
41. My Exercise Diary 104
42. Mum's New Home 107
43. Goals for 2005 110

Moving Forward
44. Mum's 79th Birthday 114
45. My Thoughts.......................................115
46. The Way Forward 117
47. 2005 Events 118
48. My Promise To Myself: 2006 122

Hurting
49. Mum's Special Birthday.........................124
50. The Party 126
51. The Dark Tunnel 128
52. Cruse Work..133
53. My Precious Mum................................135
54. Getting Away......................................141
55. Hurting Myself....................................142

New Start
56. Life without Mum 145
57. Moving to Canada – would I be better off?............148
58. Returning To Work 152
59. First Anniversary of Mum's Death 157
60. Christmas...159

61. New Year...161
62. Family Death 163
63. Summer 2008..165
64. The illness taking over 169

Last Chance For Recovery
65. Hospital In-patient again 173
66. Back to Work..199
67. My Battle With Eating at Work................200
68. 2009: Struggles with eating at work.........205
69. Losing my Friend....................................206
70. Present Day..207
71. Treatment..210

Special mention to the following;..................212

CHILDHOOD

Veronica Foster

1. Introduction

I developed my eating disorder at quite a late age. Later than what is usually expected, according to most professionals. I was in fact past my teen years, but when I look back into these years there were signs of me having an eating disorder. I use the term "eating disorder," not Anorexia, not Bulimia. I existed somewhere along the spectrum of disorders neither here nor there a non-specific case, not easily defined.

My life was not filled with any horror stories, or anything that was shocking. My parents were caring and loving and they did the best they could for us. I don't think that I would be the person I am today if it wasn't for them.

My story is for those out there who may not understand what eating disorders are really about. They are not about diets, weight or even food! This may appear to be a massive contradiction, but my eating disorder is used to block out emotional problems. It blocks out feeling so much that I do not feel anything. I am not someone who walks around feeling sorry for myself, seeking to gain attention, but I am simply a person unable to deal with my emotional problems, so I deal with them through food.

I have had four hospital admissions; I have seen six therapist and counting, I have attended eating disorder support groups. I am understanding more about my illness and working through it every day, through the help of the professional workers.

2. My Childhood

I was born in Sorrento Maternity Hospital, Birmingham on the 13th October 1966. My first home was Durham Road Sparkhill. I lived there for the first 3 months of my life, and then moved to my second home when my dad brought a house a few miles away. I am the youngest of 3 with 2 older brothers.

My parents arrived in England in the 1950s from Jamaica. My Dad came first in 1959, and my mum arrived later the same year. They had not met before, but they attended the same church in Sparkhill, Birmingham; they fell in love and then later got married.

My childhood memories are vivid; I remember having to spend a lot of my time with my godmother because my mum had a lot of hospital admissions due to a long term illness she had. I know that as a child I was often scared. When you are that young, 3-5 years old, you need to feel secure and loved and I felt I never got that when I was left in my godmother's house. My memories of being left with her aren't happy ones - I just wanted to be with my mum.

I attended Springfield Infants and Junior School. I had many friends at school, but my best friend was Jodie, and she remained my friend throughout my school life.

Mum brought me to school on the first day. I liked school when I was in the Infants, for it was good fun. The teachers were really nice and I remember playing in the Wendy house, making cups of tea and playing outside on the bikes and having story time with the teachers and the rest of my classmates. I also remember my first reading book, Peter and Jane. Those were the good days.

My brothers George and Mark were always very protective of me because I was the youngest and also being a girl, they looked after me and they were always very kind and gentle towards me. I remember my brother George would always tease me and call me 'Picky Head' (that was a childhood name from Jamaica; I knew that he only did it in fun).

3. Puberty Trouble

All through my childhood. God had been an important part of my life. My parents brought me up in a local church, nearby.

I remember my dad going to regular prayer meetings at people's houses; I also remember every Sunday morning having worship time at home where we would read from the Bible, sing and then pray, although I would sometimes fall asleep in the mornings. My parents were strong Christians and had a big impact on me through my childhood and into my adult life.

I enjoyed my school life until I reached the age of 9, when I started to feel disgusted with my body and the way I looked. I believe it was because at this age I started my periods, but I didn't have a clue about what was going on. I only remember my mum taking me to the doctor's because I don't think she knew what was going on either, but the doctor explained what was happening.

I remember looking at my body with my big boobs and fat tummy; I just looked ugly and felt ugly too. All my friends looked nice and I wanted to look like them. I couldn't even explain what was happening to them. This was a hard time for me, tummy ache, being sick and feeling disgusted with my body. I don't know how I managed to get through primary school feeling like this, and it didn't get any easier in secondary school, the feelings about my body. I remember always hiding away in the changing rooms getting changed for P.E, because I didn't want anyone to see my fat, ugly body and my big boobs - I've always hated them. The way I felt about my body affected my self-esteem a lot through my teen years. I always felt different from my friends.

I had some good friends in school; some closer to me than others. I was always the one in the group of friends that had to do the stupid things like throwing stones at school windows or leaving school at lunch time without permission. These were all things that I did to impress my friends and to be part of the little gangs we used to have.

There were 1 or 2 girls in the group I used to hang around with, and I used to be very close to - one girl went to the same branch of church as me, (I went to the church in Acocks Green), and she went to the one in Shard End. Our parents knew each other very well; we used to meet up at our church conventions at our town hall. When we used to meet up, we would spend most of the time outside instead of inside joining in with the worship. It was good fun, and I used to really enjoy going to conventions - that was the only thing I had to look forward to, since we didn't have a lot of family outings.

The other friend that I was close to was in my class. I sat with her in most of our lessons and we would meet each other in the mornings before school. Mum and dad never liked me to hang around with people that didn't go to church, so none of my friends ever came round to my house, and I was not allowed to go to theirs. I was never allowed to go to the park to meet them. I often thought my parents were very over-protective. I think they were strict parents because of their strong church beliefs and they brought us up in the church environment. Whereas most of my peers had been a lot younger; about 7 years old. Both of my brothers were younger than me.

I decided to become a member of the church when I was about 14 years, whereas most children had become members at 7 or 8 years old. I always felt that I never did anything right; I was never as good as my peers from church, school or family. This was probably because of the way I felt about my body, which made me feel that I was never good enough.

4. My Early Years
Home Life

I felt that I never had a close relationship with my parents during my school years. This may have been because my dad had to work extra hard due to my mum always being unwell; physically she was the weaker one and I never really, as a child, spent any time with mum. Even when we went to church, we would walk with dad while mum always waited for another church member to come and give her a lift to church. We would go on day trips to seaside resorts once a year, usually just with dad. Mum used to come occasionally, but doing a lot of walking was hard for her.

At home mum would do all the cooking and cleaning; I suppose that would be the right role for a woman in the 70s and 80s. I never had a problem with food in my childhood; I can't remember ever being a fussy eater.

In our culture, meals played a big part. We would have invites from church friends to visit their homes on Sunday afternoons for dinner. The main meal would always be rice and peas and chicken with roast potatoes, vegetables, and macaroni cheese and afters. I always thought that I was a lot fatter than my peers - I always hated my body, and I would have the odd comment from others that I was big, but this never really had an impact on me.

My mum loved cooking, and she was always in the kitchen cooking something - rice and peas and chicken with roast potatoes, sweet corn and salad. I loved liver and turn corn meal (this was one of my favourite meals), and the Caribbean soups that she used to make. There was always a lovely smell coming from the kitchen in our house. Mum made delicious cakes; she tried to teach me, but I couldn't make them half as well as she did. I was always amazed that mum never measured her ingredients, but they always came out perfect. To this day I don't know how she did that.

We had really good neighbours, on both sides. On one side was an elderly lady, and on the other side was a family with kids who were the same age as me and my brothers. We would play in each others' gardens, which was really good. Our parents would often be in the garden talking to each other. One thing that I noticed about my parents from an early age was that they didn't just say they were Christians, they acted like Christians and would be there whenever our neighbours needed help.

When I attended church, there were a lot of families with young children. I often became involved with these children through playing with them after the service and sometimes I would take an interest in them from day one by visiting them when they were born. One of the leaders asked me if I would be interested in helping her on a Sunday - I said "yes" and I loved it ever since. Working in Children's Church was like being in church, but it was at the children's level of understanding. It involved teaching the children about church and God.

While I was working with the children in Children's Church I realised how I was able to reach out to them at their level, how they interacted with me, and how much I enjoyed being with them and teaching them too. I was then asked to be a Sunday school teacher for the 2-5 year olds, in the 'Kindergarten class'. I just loved this class as I got so much from the children, who were like sponges. I came every week with new lessons and they would just take everything in. They loved it. It was brilliant being a Sunday school teacher, I learnt so much from that time. I saw for myself how much I could reach out to young children, and how I really interacted with them. I also got to work with babies in another role.

Through my work with the children in church, I decided that I would pursue a career with children. The interesting thing about my work with them was that my dad also had a Sunday school class, though the children he worked with were a bit older, 8-10 year olds. My Dad drew children to him because he had a brilliant personality and he was a fun person to be around because he always made people laugh, which children especially appreciated.

The involvement of my mum and dad in the church had a big impact in my life. My dad was also a Band Leader, one of the Pastor's assistants (he was in charge of a small group of people, and was there for them if they needed help and advice). Dad enjoyed raising funds for church too. Mum was not as active as dad because of her health, but she never let that stop her from worshipping her God. The way we grew up was very restricted

8

and strict. I did not understand it at the time, but as I got older I have grown to understand and appreciate it.

5. My Career

When I told my parents about my decision to work in child care, I'm not sure whether they were happy for me. I believe they thought it wasn't much of a career, wiping children's noses! They wanted me to be a nurse or a secretary because in the 70s and 80s they were the jobs to have and nobody in church was doing childcare. My peers weren't going into jobs like childcare, which was another reason why I felt as though I was always being compared to others around me. I was constantly being compared unfavorably to what my family, church members and peers were doing. Sometimes I wished that I was praised and encouraged more for the talents and abilities that I had. I always felt that I was compared with how my peers dressed, appeared and their talents, which always made me feel not good enough, never being good at anything I did. I think that this may be typical for some black families who do not praise their children.

My parents came round to my decision to work with children in the end, however. My dad did try one more thing in order to persuade me otherwise, by buying me a typewriter. I learnt how to use it, but I stuck with my decision to work with children.

I managed to finish school, though I didn't enjoy the final year at all. I just couldn't wait to finish. I left school with 5 GCSE's, and I started to work towards my career in childcare by getting into a local college, at City and Guilds, studying Home Economics for Family and Community Care.

6. Siblings

My brother, George, got married when I was 14 years old and he was 22. My mum and dad were so proud of him. It was a lovely wedding, the sun shone all day, and it was just a thoroughly enjoyable day.

My brother George was always a hard worker. He was always studying, with his books open, working hard. I think that if he had gone to university he would have got a degree; he should have gone on to university. He was always helping mum around the house with everything - housework, shopping and cleaning. George also liked to play the piano and organ; I remember when he played the organ in church. He was a very good runner. He belonged to a big Birmingham running club, and also ran for the school. George was 8 years my senior and would always give me advice; as a big brother he was always protective over me.

My brother Mark was different. He was more outgoing; and he had a lot of friends. I think George had some school friends but I don't remember him ever having a close friend. He did have one close friend at church, however. Mark had loads of friends. I think out of the three of us, he was the most popular; he would always be out and about with his mates. He too played the big brother role very well, and would try to protect me and look after me.

As a family, we never really shared any feelings with each other; I think that was due to the fact that mum and dad were very reserved people, who never shared their feelings or thoughts with anyone. Mum was very quiet, and dad never took anything seriously - he never let anything bother him, everything was a joke. If I was worried about anything, he would tell me to "Go find work to do" (in the true Jamaican way!). I never saw him letting anything or anyone bother him.

ADOLESCENT YEARS

7. College Life

My career in childcare began at college; I really enjoyed the 2 year course. We were also taught about elderly care, and I got a chance to go into care homes, but I didn't enjoy this part of the course. I also went into special schools, which I found enjoyable but challenging. My course also enabled me to go into infant schools. Although I wanted to do this I didn't enjoy my time at the school I went to. My favourite placements were in a hospital on a ward, and a nursery placement.

Mandy taught child development, and I looked forward to her lessons the most; for her sessions were interesting, enjoyable and great fun. Mandy made herself approachable, and if any of us had any problems, or if we didn't understand anything we could ask her. She would go out of her way to help. I lived quite near to Mandy, and she would often give me a lift home. We talked about college and general everyday things, like television, music and football. Mandy would invite me round to her house at weekends where we would just relax together.

Although I really enjoyed college I did begin to see the early signs of what is now an eating disorder, because there would be days when I wouldn't eat anything if I was stressed out or worried about something. I recall one of my tutors commenting on it, and he would be a bit worried about it. I never thought anything about it at the time, however.

I was successful at college and I passed my City and Guilds in Home Economics in Family and Community Care. My mum and dad were pleased with me for doing well in college but they always found it hard to really say what they thought, mainly because they themselves were never praised by their parents when they were growing up. I gained a lot of self-confidence during my college years for the first time. I was happier, and I didn't feel so different to my friends.

My relationship with my parents began to grow at this stage in my life; whilst at college, I had grown up a lot and I was successful at college, although I would always be my mum and dad's baby, no matter how old I was. My mum was the strongest of the family. My dad was a factory manual worker for many years. Mum found a job working in a local chemist where she worked for a few years. She enjoyed this job and they all loved her at work.

The most wonderful thing that my mum would say to me when I was going through any difficult times in my life was that she would tell me that she was praying for me, or she would just encourage me in the way that she knew. Mum would always be singing around the house; she loved her family and she would do anything for them.

Sunday mornings were busy in our house. The day would start at 8 o'clock when we would wake up for Sunday morning worship. Church started at 10:30am on a Sunday morning, and mum, dad and I would always be the first ones there waiting at the front gate before church was open; we were always there by 10:20am. Even though, by this time mum and dad were in their 50s/60s, they would be at every meeting - that was devotion. They also worked hard to raise money to support the church. Mum and dad would attend church as often as they could for God was at the centre of their lives.

I also started to take driving lessons while I was at college. I found this hard at first but my dad kept on encouraging me, being more enthusiastic than me about learning to drive.

8. Life After College

By the time I had finished college, I had become, for the first time, an aunt. George had the first of three daughters, Sandra, and because she was the first grandchild we were all so proud of her.

Whilst at college and during my early working life, I never went on diets or worried about my weight in any way. I never went to the gym until I was about 23 years old. I struggled to accept my body, but I always thought that I was big and fat, and I always hated the way I looked. I thought that nothing I bought ever looked right on me. I always thought my friends looked better than me at church or work.

I worked in two local nurseries as a crèche assistant for a year and then as a playgroup assistant. I enjoyed these jobs very much and they taught me a lot in my early career with children. Whilst I was working as a playgroup assistant, I passed my driving test, making my dad and mum really pleased. I think that my dad was more excited than I was for he went out and helped me buy my first car. It certainly made a difference to my confidence, being on the road driving to work instead of catching the bus. It also helped during the week for any church meetings.

I became very keen on gospel music. I started buying gospel music once I started working, and I found the music very uplifting. I also started working for a record company that used to sell albums. I would go to concerts and sell records; I enjoyed doing this a lot.

I went to a lot of gospel concerts, especially when the American artists used to perform in this country. It was brilliant, and I had a great time at these concerts. I was always inspired by gospel music because of its message of hope. I would spend hours listening to this music in my room.

Another niece was born, George's second child, June. As a family we all attended the same church, so I used to see George and his kids every Sunday and he would always come round to visit us most weekends. My mum's youngest brother attended also with his family, so I saw my uncle and my cousins every week. I guess that the whole church was a bit of a family because there were many families who were related to each other one way or another.

I worked as a part-time playgroup assistant for two years, and after that I went to work at a day nursery as a nursery officer. I enjoyed this job because it was full-time and I had more challenges. I had a good relationship with the staff, and I had my own small group of children to work with which I enjoyed a lot.

We had good news in the family during my time at the day nursery, for Mark had met and fallen in love with Marcia, and they decided to get married. I was so happy for Mark, but I was now worried that I would be left at home with my mum and dad, who were now getting frail.

I was going to be a bridesmaid at Mark and Marcia's wedding, but I felt fat and I thought I would not look nice in the dress. When the big day finally came everyone looked nice except me. I'm sure I was the fattest bridesmaid there out of all of them. It was quite a big wedding, and mum and dad were really proud of them. They had the best start to their married life that they could have had.

It was shortly after my brother Mark's wedding that my dad's health began to deteriorate. He developed Type 2 diabetes, and managed it fine at first, being able to continue with his job, but after a few months we could see that he was struggling, and starting to slow down. Dad had been a very fit person, walking for miles; he walked to work and back for years, and that was a good 30 minute walk, each way. Then most evenings, he would visit a church member, which would usually be another 30 minute walk, there and back. Dad now decided to retire and when he did his health went with it, for he developed Type 1 Diabetes, making him insulin-dependent. Dad had to go into hospital for a short time for the Doctors to sort out the amount of insulin he would need on a daily basis. They also gave me and mum a run-down on what types of foods he could eat etc. It was at this stage that I realised that mum and dad needed a lot of support because their health was deteriorating. I knew this would be a big task.

9. Dad and Mum's Health

When dad came home from the hospital, he managed his diabetes on his own as best as he could, and mum always made sure he ate correctly. Dad struggled with the insulin because at first he needed to have it twice a day. He couldn't cope with doing the insulin on his own, but he did his best; he was so used to being an independent person and the 'Bread winner' that he just found it hard to cope with the fact that he was the one who was poorly, having to depend on others.

My mum also became ill too, having had Schizophrenia since I was about 3 years old, although she had had at least 15 years without a relapse. It was at this stage that I realised why I had spent so much time with my godmother when I was little, with mum so ill, and having to spend so much time in hospital. It was not very nice seeing her ill with such an unpleasant illness, but when mum started to take her medication she was fine. The one thing that upset me about it was that no one knew or understood the illness; no one explained what mum's illness was and how to look for the signs of a relapse or even how to help her. That was why I sometimes got annoyed with the team that treated her. If I had I known a bit more about the problem, it wouldn't have been such a big shock.

10. My First Holiday

I worked at the day nursery for about 18 months. I then applied for another position at another children's centre. This involved working in a bigger setting alongside teachers; I thought that this would be a better place to work as I would learn more by working alongside teachers.

I remember my first day, when I came to work at my new job. I was introduced to Fiona, who had just come back from maternity leave, for her first child. Fiona was a great person to work with because she was loud and lovely and she would always tell you to your face what she thought. When I arrived the first thing she said was, "My name is Fiona. I have just come back from maternity leave after having a little girl. Don't worry about anything, I feel quite new myself at the moment. I will take care of you." I thanked her for making me feel at ease, and relaxed. Fiona then showed me around. I was with 2—3 year olds; I learnt the basics like the daily routine. I was introduced to the other staff and the children and parents. I felt part of the nursery quite quickly.

I decided to take my first holiday abroad not long after arriving at the nursery; in fact this was the first holiday I had ever taken. I decided to go to America to see one of my cousins, but my parents were not impressed, and didn't want me to go at all, but I wrote to my cousin Tony, in America, and he was more than happy for me to come. I went to Boston in the fall (autumn) and it was beautiful. I had a fantastic time out there. I met Tony and his wife, Gail, and their 2 boys, a toddler and a baby. They were lovely. I met Gail's cousin while I was there; she too had come over from England on a holiday, so we spent the day together, and we had a nice time shopping. We also spent a day in New York, sightseeing.

I had my 25th Birthday in America, and I remember feeling a little homesick. Boston was just lovely in the fall, and I had never seen the colour of leaves like that before. I didn't want to come home. I met one of my cousin's relatives while I was in Boston and we spent the day together; we visited a Sealife Centre and we went out for a meal together. I just could not believe that I had got on a plane by myself and travelled all the way to America to visit one of my cousins, whom I did not know that well, and it was a big achievement.

I became an Auntie again, not long after my holiday, when Mark and Marcia had the first of 3 children, Sean. When Marcia went into hospital to have him, her mum rang our house and she wanted to go to the hospital to see Marcia, for she was really worried about her because it was her firstborn, so I went to her house to see her and then maybe go to the hospital. We waited for a phone call, but then we decided to go to the hospital anyway. When we arrived he had not long been born so they let us in and he was just lovely; my first nephew.

11. Dad's Health

I arrived home one evening and one of the neighbours approached me and told me that dad had had a fall on the street, and that he had been taken to hospital. When I asked her what had happened, she said that he was going shopping and then she saw him on the floor. She and her husband managed to get him up and bring him to the house; they first called mum, then they called for an ambulance because he had cut his face really badly and was bleeding a lot. I got to the hospital as quickly as I could; when I saw my dad, his face was really bad; I was really shocked for he was in a real mess. I asked my dad what happened, but he didn't remember. I spoke to the nurse and they thought the he had had a blackout which was probably caused by his diabetes. Dad said he had eaten his breakfast and lunch and that he had felt ok when he went out. Dad needed stitches to his face and had to stay in hospital for three days while the doctors monitored his insulin just to see if it needed to be increased.

When dad came home the district nurses came out every day to give him his medicated insulin.

We all kept a close eye on him but I could see that he was slowing down and wasn't coping very well. Three weeks after he had had the fall he had another setback; he had to go into hospital again, for he had had a minor stroke and couldn't walk very well; the left side of his face was dropping slightly. He seemed to recover from this quite quickly, and was back on his feet and walking quite well. He was back at home after a 2 week stay in hospital, which was really good.

12. Grandad

My mum and dad looked after their grandson, Sean, for the first 2 years of his life every day. Dad loved having Sean, playing football with him, taking him shopping, or just holding him and talking to him. They both really enjoyed looking after Sean; I could see that dad just adored him. Sean loved them both too; as soon as he saw them he would say "Grandad" and "Grandma". When Sean was 2 years and 6 months old he went to nursery in the day because he needed more attention, being a very clever little boy. When he finished nursery, I would go and collect him and bring him to the house; then Marcia would come and collect him after work.

That was a special time for dad, and I could see how happy he was having Sean around him. However, his health wasn't the best, and he couldn't really be trusted to walk down to the shops on his own because he just couldn't cope with it. When he went to the local shops my godfather often saw him and went over to talk to him; his wife then sat him in the car and got him a drink and something to eat, for dad's insulin could not be controlled. I know for a fact that mum would always cook for him and make him sit down to have his meals and he always left the house with biscuits in his pockets or an orange or something sweet. Dad had his insulin every day because the district nurses came out to give it to him, but Ididn't really understand what was going on.

MY BODY SHAPE

13. Dad's Stroke

Things seemed to have settled down for a few months during the summer of 1993. It was in June that he had had his fall in the street and a minor stroke in the July, and the rest of the summer was spent at home trying to take it easy. Dad spent a lot of time in the garden, which was something he enjoyed doing. He would spend hours in the summer growing his own vegetables, such as potatoes, carrots, lettuce, cabbages etc. I used to love the strawberries in the garden, and I was always going out in the summer, picking and eating them. Dad did a lot of work in his garden that summer, well the best he could, and in the autumn when it became a bit cool, he was alright, and continued to go to church. It was a bit easier because I had a car, and I drove him around most of the time, either to church or to visit church friend's houses. When I wasn't around they went occasionally on the bus to town or to the shops when dad was feeling well enough. Dad's diabetes seemed to be settling down, so we all thought he was fine, and life was as normal as it could be.

I thought to myself how strange all this was because dad was always the strong one, happy and active; he never let anything worry him and he was the bread winner, but now he was the one my mum was looking after, and the one that I was most concerned about. It was really strange, and it was hard for my dad too, but I could see that he made the best of things. He continued to do the things he enjoyed and he made the best of it. He didn't want the fuss, he hated it.

Then on 6th December 1993, I was woken by my mum, who told me to come quickly for dad couldn't get out of bed. I went into the room to try to help, but I couldn't help - he was just stiff; he said he couldn't feel the left side of his body and that he couldn't feel his right leg either. So I panicked and ran downstairs to call for an ambulance. My mum told me to also phone Mark, and when he came he couldn't help move dad either. The ambulance crew arrived 30 minutes after I called them, and they took him to the local hospital, where he was examined and was admitted to the ward.

When I managed to have a chat with one of the doctors, he said that dad had had a stroke which affected his right side, and that all me and mum could do was to wait and see how he would respond to treatment. On the 9th December 1993, a few days after dad had had the stroke, Mark and Marcia had their second child, a girl, Jane. After what happened to dad this was really good news. I rang the hospital and the nurses told my dad. When we went to visit him in the evening he was so happy to hear that he was a grandad again.

The next few days were very hard for dad, who couldn't feed himself because he had lost the use of his right arm, and who couldn't even move his right leg. I could see how hard it all was for him, for he was a broken man. Dad had visitors while in hospital, who all tried to encourage him, and prayed with him too which he appreciated. I brought my mum every night to visit him, but most of the time my mum would visit him on her own, during the day. She would cook a meal and bring it up to the hospital and help him to eat it, and then come home on her own, and would wait to visit him again later in the evening, which I thought was amazing because she remained so physically and mentally strong.

After 2 weeks in the hospital, dad was moved to a rehab hospital because the doctor said he needed help to use the right side of his body. I didn't have a clue where the hospital was, but my godfather went with me to show me where it was. The hospital was not as busy, and the nurses had more time to talk to us. It was a hospital that was mainly for elderly patients, and they were able to do a lot of rehab work with dad during the day.

While all this was going on, I managed at work the best I could. People at work supported me, giving me time off to visit dad when I needed it. I had no social life outside work, for I was too busy and was always tired. It was hard work during the day, coming home and having dinner and then getting ready to visit dad every night. Also there was a 40 minute drive to get there. It was difficult because everyone would ask how dad was, and all I could say was that he was the same. Visiting him every day, they expected me to say that he managed to stand up or that he had the feeling back in his right arm and leg again, but that was never the case. I would ask the nurses how he was getting on, and they would say progress was very slow, but that dad was working very hard and was trying his best.

That year Christmas was very hard and felt strange.

Usually Christmas Day would be a family day with me, mum and dad, then Boxing Day would be with everyone -George, Kelly, Sandra, June, Mark, Marcia and Sean, (and for the first time this year, Jane).Also mum's nieces would come round with their kids and then uncle and his wife. However, this Christmas we visited dad, and spent the day there; we visited every day during the Christmas and New Year holiday, and although the family did come round on Boxing Day, it wasn't the same.

Over the next weeks nothing changed – dad spent 5 weeks in a rehab hospital, but never got the use of his right side back again and he started to feel down about it. It really upset me when I visited dad and he would break down. I saw it more when a church minister or my uncle visited him, because he would get so upset. It is really hard when you have been independent all your life, and then you can't even feed yourself or go to the toilet on your own.

One night, when I and mum visited dad, one of the nurses told me that the nurse in charge wanted to see us, so we made an appointment to see her the next evening. I don't know what I expected this nurse to say to us, but at the meeting the nurse in charge said that dad would not improve and that he would most likely spend the rest of his life in a wheelchair. I was in shock, and asked what had been happening with the rehab. She told me that he had been trying really hard, and the nurses and physiotherapist had been doing a lot of work with him and had tried really hard, but there had been no improvement. When the nurse then asked me and mum how we would cope with him at home, mum told her that we would be fine. I think the nurse was trying to say that we wouldn't be able to cope with him, but we then went on to talk about home improvements.

I was in so much shock after that meeting; we went back to dad and just sat, not saying a word. I know that dad wasn't making any improvement but I always thought that he would somehow get better, so all this was too much to take in. I knew there would have to be a lot of changes at home and that dad would have to sleep downstairs, but I don't think mum realised just how much work it was going to be. I guess all we could do was to try our best because dad wanted to be at home. When we told George, Mark and the rest of the family, I think everyone stayed positive to help us. Someone told me that dad would be alright, and that he could live for a few years in a wheelchair. They said he had only had a stroke, and people can live for years like that. I tried to remain positive for the sake of my mum, and I didn't want to upset my dad.

The hospital provided a social worker who met with us to talk to us about how we felt about dad coming home. Dad said he wanted to come home, and my mum wanted him home too because she was the one who was going to look after him and because she loved him. She wasn't going to have it any other way, and I am and will always be, so proud of her for the way she handled this situation.

I thought that I needed a bit of time to do something for myself because I had spent a lot of time at the hospital. All I was doing was going to work, and then going home to get ready to go out again to visit dad. I just wanted to do something for myself, so I thought I would join my local leisure centre. I joined the gym on the 25th January 1994, to get fit, for I knew I was overweight and I needed to lose some weight.

14. Diet and Gym

I joined the gym and I had my induction which took an hour. I went down on a Tuesday night at 7pm which was Ladies Only session; I enjoyed the workout session, so I decided to stick with it, attending on Tuesdays and Thursday evenings at 7pm. I enjoyed the sessions and I had made a few new friends. It became a real distraction from what was going on with Dad, and I also began to see the benefits of exercising for my clothes became looser after 4 weeks of training. I started to look at the sorts of foods I'd been eating and I cut back on all the rubbish in my diet like sweets, crisps, fizzy pop, pizza etc. This made me feel so much better; I had a lot more energy, and I felt a whole lot fitter.

On the nights that I was going to the gym, mum still managed to visit dad at the hospital, getting a lift with either my godfather or uncle. Dad still didn't make any progress; he was still having some physiotherapy, but it was not as much as he was having before. We had a meeting with the social worker, the nurse in charge, and the home care team about dad returning home, which dad and mum both wanted. They both continued to say that things would be alright, but they both knew that things would be hard. The social worker and the home care team arranged a day to visit our house to look at what needed to be done to help dad to return home. A social worker and the physiotherapist came to visit; they looked around and told us what they could do, saying that they would look at the front steps and that dad would have to sleep downstairs. They ordered a bed, commode and a wheelchair, but this all seemed to take a long time to sort out. I was worried about how this was going to work out, because I would be around but only in the evenings. Yes, church friends and relatives would come and help, but mum was going to be the one who would have all the pressure and hard work on her shoulders.

I continued to go to the gym, and was enjoying doing my workouts. After 6 weeks I weighed myself for the first time in years - I weighed 12 stones 13 pounds. I was shocked about this and I thought this was far too heavy for someone of my height. I must have been twice that weight before I had started going to the gym. I still went to the gym twice a week and I had gone on a diet, being really careful about what I was eating at home and at work. Now that I was weighing myself every week, I began to see the weight dropping off, and my clothes were far too big for me now - I had to buy new ones. I started off being a size 16 in tops and 14 in bottoms, so it was a great feeling buying size 12 bottoms. I would never wear trousers because I always felt too big in them, so I felt so good being able to buy jeans to look ok in them. By now, everyone at church and work was noticing that I was losing weight and they were saying I was looking good.

The social worker sent someone out from her team to look at the front stairs for wheelchair access, to see if there was anything they could do. They weren't very hopeful about it because it was going to be a big job. There was one meeting with mum's mental health team and with the hospital team, who went through the care that dad would need and the amount of support the hospital could give us. They all continued to advise us about the amount of care he would need. They also talked about respite care, which would be arranged for mum. We were all looking forward to dad's return home now, because his equipment began to arrive: his bed, his commode and his wheelchair.

Everything was in place, and we were just waiting for a discharge date for dad. I began going to the gym on a Saturday morning for an hour, because it meant that I could do more during the day. I went out and brought new scales to weigh myself with, and I watched with delight the weight going down, from 12 stone 13 pounds to 12 and ½ stones then to 12 stones. I started my diet in January, and by June I weighed 10 stones 8 pounds, which was excellent. I was now weighing myself every day to see if I was losing weight; it was good to be losing, but if I didn't lose then I would get worried and eat less; I wouldn't eat a small meal at work, but only have a drink. The comments still kept on coming from people saying that I had lost weight, that I looked really nice, and that it really suited me, which made me feel really good about everything. Although I was really worried about dad, I just didn't want to think about it all the time -I needed to escape from it all.

We had a discharge date for dad, but we had one more meeting with the social worker first. My mum and dad went over the discharge plan, since all the equipment was now at home. The district nurses would be coming in every morning to give dad his insulin and to get him dressed and out of bed, and in the evenings the home care team would come to get him dressed and put him back into bed. Respite would happen as and when we needed it, and dad would also go to a Day Care Centre every Wednesday to do some activities.

15. Dad Comes Home

So the day for discharge finally came, and I watched from mum and dad's room as dad came home in an ambulance. As I watched them take him out of the van in the wheelchair, I started crying for it was just so hard to see him coming home in a wheelchair; he was always my hero. Things were difficult, and dad was very demanding, calling mum for every little thing, even at night, but she just wanted to help him as much as she could. Shortly after dad came home, mum had to go into hospital, with really swollen legs, and they thought she had a blood clot, so dad had to go into respite care. I was really worried about mum and dad; I was visiting mum in hospital and dad at respite. Mum was given treatment and was discharged, having some time to recover at home before dad was to come home.

Dad managed to go back to church, although it took a few men to get him in the van and into church. I found the church visits very emotional, and I burst into tears. I know dad found it hard, and he was very moved to.

There were times at home when I would get frustrated; I don't think it was always about dad calling for mum all the time or mum doing too much, I think it was the whole set-up and the way things now were. The church members would come and help mum, and Uncle and Auntie would come every week to see mum, as did my godfather and his wife. It was never ideal, but my mum was a star, and she did her very best.

The diet was going really well, and I was still losing weight, although it was not as much as I wanted to lose. I started to weigh myself first thing in the morning, then straight after I had eaten something, and then as soon as I got home from work. I would eat my evening meal, then straight afterwards I would weigh myself again; finally, I would weigh myself just before I went to bed. I felt that I had to do this every day, and kept a record of my weight; if it increased, I would reduce my intake; which was getting less and less every week. I stopped eating at work altogether, because I didn't need to eat during the day and most of the food at the nursery was weight-gaining food anyway, so I didn't want to eat at work or even drink anything. I also became very fussy about what I ate at home, eating steamed fish all the time, and also chicken and sweet corn, macaroni & cheese and vegetable soup. I had to eat by 6pm, and I refused to eat after that time.

At the weekends I would have to go down to the local chemist and weigh myself there because I knew the scales there were really accurate. I don't think anyone noticed I was losing weight, but I continued to get comments like "you're looking good, are you on a diet"? I would just say "yes" because I was on a diet and I was feeling really good.

My mum and I continued looking after dad, although mum was doing most of the work. She had a wonderful spirit and she kept her faith in God though all this. I still went to church and I still did my Sunday school teaching which was great. The children all responded to me and they were all learning, and enjoying my class. Mum wasn't able to attend church as often as she used to because she never wanted to leave dad. One Sunday we did leave him, because he said he would be "ok," but we only went to church for 2 hours, and couldn't wait to get back home to see if he was alright. He was fine when we returned home, and he couldn't understand why we were making such a fuss.

The grandchildren still came round to see us; Sandra and June came with their dad, and Sean and Jane would also come. Dad enjoyed having them round, and watching them play. Jane was very young, only about 9 months old, so she didn't know dad that much. We all thought that things were settling down again, with dad's health stable; it was now December, and we were all starting to think about Christmas. I was worrying about my diet and how I was going to get through Christmas, with all the food and the eating. But then dad took a turn for the worse.

16. Dad's Relapse

One day I arrived home from work, but as soon as I got in, mum told me that dad was not well again, for he had been very confused during the day and his face looked as if it had dropped. I phoned the doctor, and when he arrived he examined dad. He thought that he might have had a minor stroke, so he phoned for an ambulance to take him to the hospital. Dad went into hospital on the 12th December 1994, two weeks before Christmas.

This was mine and mum's second Christmas without dad at home. Christmas was really quiet as we spent half the day with dad and the other half with the family. On Boxing Day we had George and his family and Mark & his family round, and I spent most of the time with the kids. At dinner time, I tried some of the food, turkey with roast potatoes, sprouts, white rice and gravy. Mum used to cook lots of food when everyone came round; 6 families would never be able to eat all the food mum cooked, so everyone always enjoyed their Boxing Day dinner with us.

Dad's hospital was quite near to us, so there was not much travelling to do, and it took me only 10-15 minutes to get there. Dad was making slight improvements; his face wasn't as lean as when he first arrived in hospital, and he appeared to have made some recovery. The nurses didn't seem to be too concerned about him, although they did say that he had had another small stroke. We all kept our hopes up, and we prayed that he would make a quick recovery and be home again soon.

My diet continued, and I was now 9 stones 7 pounds, which I thought was still too big for my height. I just wanted to be 9 stones, so I started to go to the gym for longer. I still went to the Ladies Only gym session on Tuesday and Thursday nights but I would get there at 6:30pm on those nights; the Ladies Only sessions started at 7pm. I would use that extra half an hour to do more workouts in the gym. I increased my workouts to include Saturday mornings- I would go in the morning and do an hour and a half, using weights and the cardio machine in the hope that I would achieve my set goal of 8 ½ stone.

In February 1995, the doctors called me and mum in for a meeting, to talk to us about dad, for he was looking better, and they were thinking about sending him home. When the doctors asked us how we felt about this, again mum said she would be happy if dad returned. We told the doctors what had already been set up for dad at home, and they were happy with everything, so they said that since dad was looking better he would be returning home soon.

Then on Friday 11th February 1995, dad took a turn for the worse. He was just lying on the bed not moving as if he was unconscious. I spoke to the nurse and she said that they all thought that dad had had another stroke and that it was a case of us all waiting to see what would happen. That weekend was very difficult for us because he made no improvement. We let family members and church friends know what was happening; they all came to visit dad, and they encouraged mum. On the Sunday when we visited dad, he was still the same, not moving, and still unconscious. I was very worried now and mum was too. I didn't sleep at all that night; I just tossed and turned all night thinking about dad. On the Monday morning mum said to me that she had to go to the doctor's and I said that I would go into work and phone the hospital to see if there was any change.

I set off for work and set up the nursery. When I informed the other staff that my dad was ill and that I needed to phone the hospital to see how he was, they all were very supportive. I phoned the ward, and the nurse said that she had been trying to call us at home to tell us that dad's condition was getting worse. I told her that my mum was at the doctor's, but I would go and pick her up and we would be there as soon as we could. I went back and informed the staff, and a very close friend (Rosie) drove me in her car to get mum. It was hard to tell mum that dad was ill and that the hospital had been desperately trying to get in touch with us. Mum just rushed out of the doctor's surgery with me and Rosie, and we drove to the hospital. When we got there we ran over to dad, to find that his breathing was bad. The nurse told us he was ill and it didn't look very good, so I phoned Mark and my uncle, and they both came quickly to the hospital.

That day seemed really long. Dad's breathing was bad, and he was in a lot of pain, finding it hard to get his breath. News soon got around that dad was ill, so the Pastor and close church friends came to the hospital to see him. The doctor came down and he had a chat with me, mum and Mark about dad, telling us what we already knew. It took me by surprise when Mark said that he didn't know how I was coping and that I was very strong; I didn't know he thought that way about me. The doctor told us that he didn't think my dad would make it through the night, for he had pneumonia which was why his breathing was so bad. It was hard to take it in that dad's life was coming to an end.

That evening the hospital ward was full of visitors for dad. I don't think he knew how many people were there, or even who they were. Church people came to pray, and my godfather and his wife came; my godfather's wife took both me and mum downstairs to get something to eat. I didn't want to go but she insisted; she said I bet you haven't eaten anything all day; and to be honest the last thing I was thinking of was food and drink, but I did manage to eat half a sandwich- I just wanted to go back to the ward. Everyone started to go home but my auntie, Mark and his mother-in-law (Marcia's mum), me and mum stayed at the hospital through the night. At 11:30pm I was very tired; my aunt told me and Mark to take a rest in the lounge area, so we did. However it wasn't long before we were called back again. We ran back, but dad had passed away.

17. Dad's Death

My aunt went to call for a nurse, who came and examined dad, confirming that he had passed away at midnight on 14th February 1995. The room was quiet at first, and then my aunt started to cry. Mum was quiet, and Mark was quiet but you could see his eyes filling up with tears; Marcia's mum was also quiet. I just stood there staring at dad and holding his hands; the nurse wanted to do things to dad, but I just wanted him to leave dad alone. We stayed at the hospital for about an hour, and then we all left together. Mum and I came home; Mark took his mother-in-law and our aunt home, and then went to get George, for no one could get hold of him earlier. Mark must have woken them all up because by this time it was 1:30 am. George and Mark came to the house immediately, and they started to take down dad's bed, and pack away all his equipment. After we sorted that out me and mum went to bed, mum sleeping in my room with me. George came in, and we all talked together on the bed, but I must have fallen asleep, for when I woke up George had gone.

18. Saying Goodbye

The next day when I woke up it was so strange, it didn't seem real that dad was dead. When I went downstairs the living room was empty because all of dad's equipment had been taken down. Mum was making breakfast, and she asked if I wanted anything to keep my strength up, but I told her I didn't want anything; the last time I had eaten was the night before at the hospital, when all I had was half a sandwich and a drink, for I couldn't eat any more.

The phone started ringing as everyone sent their sympathies. Mark and George came round because they wanted to go to collect the death certificate; our Pastor came round too. George, Mark and I all went to the hospital; it felt strange when I arrived on the ward, and we went into the office to collect dad's clothes. I kept looking around to see if dad was still there, but of course he wasn't; it wasn't sinking in that dad was gone. We collected the certificate from the hospital, and then went to the registry office to register dad's death. When we drove over to my uncle's house, I stayed in the car, and I just kept looking at the certificate. Then we all went home; mum had some visitors, so she kept herself occupied, which was good. When one of my cousins rang, I just started crying on the phone; it all just caught up with me. The rest of the day was spent with the visitors, and we all tried to plan dad's funeral. During this time everything was a blur – I didn't go to the gym, and I couldn't eat much. I was just trying to cope and get through.

The days leading to dad's funeral were just like a dream, and it really didn't seem real - going to the undertakers to choose a coffin, arranging the funeral, people visiting the house, it was all strange. My uncle from Huddersfield came to stay with us for that week, and it was nice having him around.

On the day of the funeral some beautiful flowers arrived very early in the morning. The undertakers phoned to check if everything was ok. I wasn't sure whether Sean and Jane were going to come, because they were very young; Sean was only 3 and Jane was just 14 months. In the end they did come, but I wasn't sure how much they knew about what was going on. Sean may have understood, but I knew Jane didn't know what was going on. The cars arrived to collect the flowers; they put them in with dad's coffin, which was so sad to watch.

The funeral went really well. It was a lovely service with lots of people, speeches, a solo, and the choir sang also. The only part I didn't like was when dad's coffin was opened; it was horrible having it open all the way through the service and seeing dad lying there. I found it very difficult when George took me, mum, Uncle and Marcia's mum to visit him in the chapel of rest.

After the service, the cars took us to the grave which was at Brandwood End Cemetery; I think this was the second time I had actually gone to this graveyard. We sang a few songs while dad was being buried. Then we put flowers on the grave. I felt that a part of me was buried with my dad. I just felt so empty and sad inside. As we drove away in the cars, I looked back at dad's grave with all the flowers on it. I didn't want to leave him there all alone, in that cold place.

After the funeral we went back to the church for a meal. All I wanted to eat was a sandwich, but I remember my cousin Pamela taking the sandwich out of my hands and telling me that I needed to eat a proper meal, so I did try to eat something. Lots of people came over to talk to me; I remember that during the time dad was ill and even after dad had died, the house was always full of people, but after the funeral only a small handful of people came to visit. Although mum and I found it difficult to talk about dad, we as a family needed to talk about him. I wanted to talk about my dad all the time, because he was just a wonderful father and losing him just left me feeling so lost, and the house felt so empty without him. There was a huge hole in the family, a place that will never ever be filled. Dad had such a wicked sense of humour, and he used to have me rolling on the floor in laughter with his jokes and the things he used to come out with; nothing or nobody used to upset him or make him feel unhappy. He was my Rock. Mum really missed him, but my mum's faith helped her; my faith wasn't as strong as hers. When mum wanted to encourage me she used to say that dad had gone to heaven and that I shouldn't mourn him. I do believe that dad had gone on to a better place, but I was missing him so much; I felt so empty, angry, upset and lost without him, and I just didn't know how to deal with all these feelings. I did try to stay strong for mum because of her physical and mental health. I didn't want her to become ill, for she needed me now more than ever, and I needed her too. So we both tried to stay strong for each other. I think it was easier for Mark and George, because they both had their families to support them and take care of them, so they could get on with their lives.

19. Life After Dad's Death

The first year after dad's death was a very difficult one, and I became more and more obsessed with my diet and exercise. I stepped up my gym workouts, and was spending more and more time at the gym. I was trying to cut back on the amount of food I was eating, which made me feel good. The more I saw my weight going down on the scales the better I felt about myself. Everyone began to notice my weight loss and they started to comment on it; a work colleague told me that I had done really well with my diet but I needed to stop now because I had lost enough. I told her that I just needed to lose a few more pounds, then I would stop. I always had a goal in mind, a weight that I needed to get to. By now I had stopped eating at work altogether, and I would wait until I got home to eat a meal. I felt that one meal a day was all I needed in order to keep my weight under control and to lose even more weight.

Mum started to worry about my diet because she noticed my behaviour around food; I had to have my meal before 6pm because anything I ate after that time would mean that I would gain weight again, and that couldn't happen! I stopped weighing myself every day because I would get really frustrated when my weight didn't change or if the scales said I was gaining weight, which made me really upset. I used to get really angry and became even stricter on myself. So every Saturday morning after gym I would weigh myself and save all the tickets showing how my weight was progressing. In the first year after dad's death, my weight went down to 8 stones 7 pounds; I was so happy and I felt really proud of myself but negative comments about my weight started to happen. My mum said I was starting to look too "marga" (too thin), and friends also told me that I had lost too much weight and that I needed to stop now. I got really upset, and didn't understand why or what they were saying because, as far as I was concerned, I was fat and needed to lose more weight; my goal was now to get to 8 stones and then I could stop.

The gym was the only place where I could go to feel better. When I went to church; which I tried to continue to do, I couldn't feel anything spiritually; I was angry with God for taking my dad. I felt that my faith had become very weak, but I couldn't talk to anyone about it. I did listen to a lot of gospel music which helped me continue to believe in God and keep my faith, but I couldn't see past the fact that dad was dead. Dad went to the church that I attended all my life, being a strong and faithful member there, but all I could picture was dad's dead body lying at the front of the church in his coffin, which just haunted me.

I continued to attend church with my mum. I don't know how my mum kept going, she was so strong and her faith was amazing and she never stopped believing in God - her trust in Him never stopped. I did find it hard and strange because I felt that we never spoke about dad. I know that as Christians we should believe that when someone dies they have gone to a better place, but all I wanted to do was talk about my dad. Maybe I was scared to talk to mum about dad because I didn't want to upset her. Mum used to get angry with me if I got upset about dad, and would tell me to stop worrying and mourning my father. I think my mum was trying to hold it all in and be strong. Mum always wanted to visit dad's grave, but I found it hard to go. It was really upsetting for me to be there, but mum found it comforting.

20. My Diet Takes Over

My diet and my weight loss had become more noticeable, and friends and family members were commenting on it. I became more and more trapped into it, until I finally reached my target weight of 8 stones. I was so pleased and proud of myself, so I put my new target weight to 7 stones 7 pounds. I made my evening meals even smaller; I would have one piece of chicken and a small amount of sweet corn with a potato, and I would only have two drinks throughout the day. I also started to lie and say that I'd already eaten when I hadn't; so that everyone would stop questioning me about my meals. I wasn't happy with my weight and I hated the way my body looked; as far as I was concerned I was far too fat and I needed to be thinner, so I continued with my diet.

It was 18 months after dad's death that mum started to fall ill. Up to this point mum was really well, and seemed to be strong both physically and emotionally so I didn't have any concerns about her at all. But she suddenly started to do and say strange things, and would stay up all night walking around the house, saying strange things; I later discovered that all this behavior was a part of her condition. Mum had schizophrenia, which she had had ever since I was really young; mum had at least 15 years free from this illness because I had never seen any of the symptoms as a teenager or as a young adult, so when I did see my mum ill it was very scary because I didn't know what to do. The local mental health team came round in order to assess her, and to check whether she had been taking her medication, which I think she must have stopped doing at some stage. They managed to get mum to start taking her medication again and mum calmed down and became well again. She was assigned a community psychiatric nurse to help her and keep an eye on her, and also offer her support in the community. Mum's illness was still not explained to us as a family, which made me upset and angry. I felt that that my mum had an illness, and so she needed a lot of help. As her daughter, I needed to understand the illness- to know what it was, and be able to recognize the symptoms. When I was growing up, the only thing people said about mum's illness was that she had "nerves", which didn't mean anything to me. Saying that mum had "nerves" was another way of saying she was mad in our culture and we don't like to ask questions and try to understand illnesses.

When mum started to see her community nurse, I asked questions about her condition because I didn't understand it. When the nurse explained to me what mum's illness was, I understood it a lot more, but not well enough to recognise the signs and symptoms of its onset. It became difficult at home, and I was constantly worrying about mum, both her mental and physical health. Other people did help as best as they could by visiting us and going shopping for Caribbean food from town, but it was important that I stayed strong and was there to support mum. I wanted to be the perfect daughter for my mum because I loved her so much, and she was so precious to me. I believed she was the best mum in the whole world and she always did the best for me when I was growing up, always being caring and soft and gentle with me. I wanted to always be there for my mother, just as she had always been there for me.

I was still losing weight, which had now dropped to 7 stones 11 pounds. I was very pleased with myself, though everyone else was quite concerned for me. I had a comment from a work friend which was very hurtful- she said she thought I was looking very ill. I remember thinking at the time "How dare they say that to me, what do they know?" More comments came from the church community, for everyone now was saying something about the way I looked. I thought I was fat and needed to lose just a few more pounds, and then I would stop this diet and start eating normally again. I would even eventually start to cut back on going to the gym; of course I would still go to maintain my weight, but I would probably go three times a week instead of the six days that I was doing at the time.

I continued to diet, and started to look at slimming magazines also. I started to stay longer at the gym and cut back even further on my meals. In the evenings my meals now consisted of one piece of chicken with a small piece of sweet corn and a drink. I didn't have any breakfast, and had nothing else to eat or drink during the day. One Saturday morning, when I went to the gym for my morning workout, I did my usual workout routine - the stepper followed by the bike, the treadmill and then finally the weight machines. But half way through my exercising I started to feel really sick and dizzy, so I sat for a

42

moment, but this didn't help. I got up again to walk out of the gym, but the next thing I knew was when I opened my eyes and found myself on the floor, with the gym instructor next to me, telling me to lie still for a minute. When I sat up, she asked if I had had any breakfast, and I told her I hadn't; she then pointed out that that was why I had fainted and told me to go home and not to come back into the gym. I was quite surprised that I had passed out because I had felt fine in the morning. I didn't say anything to mum when I got home, because I didn't want her to worry about me. In a way it did scare me because I had never fainted before in my life, so I was left a bit frightened by this experience.

I continued with my diet, even after what had happened, for I still wanted to reach my target weight of 7 stones 7 pounds. At my next weigh-in, I was 7 stones 9 pounds, and I was very disappointed because I had only lost 2 pounds, so I tried to spend more time at the gym, 1½ - 2 hours, to see if this would help. I started to work more on the cardio machine, and I also enjoyed exercising on the treadmill. I didn't run, but just walked at a fast pace. I loved the stepper machine too because it showed how many steps you had taken and how many calories you had burnt off. I also enjoyed the bikes. I continued to do the weights, but not as much as I had done before, and I started to do a 'Bums & Tums' class, just to vary my exercise. I enjoyed this class but it was always hit and miss whether it happened because we either didn't have a room or the instructor didn't turn up to take the class, so joining in that class became very frustrating to me, and I decided to just stick with my workout at the gym because at least that was reliable.

I managed to reach my target weight, of 7 stones 6 pounds. I was so proud of myself that I could do it but I was still not happy with the way I looked, so I set my new target weight of 7 stones 4 pounds, which I felt would be easy, as I only had to lose 2 pounds. However, everyone at this stage was really worried about how much weight I was losing. I had really harsh comments now, like "You are starting to look anorexic". I was so upset that people said that to me. How dare they call me that, for I was not thin.

I was now getting advice to go and see a doctor because my close friends were really worried, thinking I had a big problem and that I needed help with it. I knew that my diet was getting out of control because I was never happy with the target weight I set for myself. As soon as I reached my target, I then set myself another one, while all I kept on seeing in the mirror was a fat person. I was now a size 8 in clothes, and even they were starting to hang off me, but I found that I was still hiding my body under big t-shirts and baggy jeans. I recognized that I had a problem, but I didn't think I had an eating disorder at this stage. I decided to listen to my friends and take that first step of seeing a doctor.

21. Doing As I Am Told

My visit to the doctor was very nerve-racking. When I went in I didn't know what to say, I was so nervous about what he was going to say to me. I told the doctor that I was on a diet because I needed to lose weight; this was all I said to the doctor. He then told me that I needed to take some tablets to lift my mood; so I thanked him and quickly left the room. The doctor had prescribed anti-depression tablets, which I collected from the chemist. I tried taking the tablets for a while but they didn't help. I couldn't understand why the doctor had given them to me in the first place; I knew that I wasn't really myself since my dad became ill, and during the days leading to his death. I knew I was devastated by his death, but I couldn't see how a box of tablets was going to help me. This visit made no difference at all. I only went there in the first place because I was getting so much pressure from my friends and family, and I couldn't see what all the fuss was about.

The weight loss had to continue until I was happy with my weight; then, and only then, could I continue with my life. I now made rules about my eating habits, not allowing myself to eat until 6pm, and not even allowing myself to have a drink. At first this was really hard, but I soon got used to it, and it became easy. The exercise now took up 2 and 2½ hours a day. I really enjoyed my exercise sessions as an escape from reality. I used exercise to lose weight, to shape my body, and also to block out all my emotions. At the time it helped me deal with the loss of my dad, which was a very fresh emotion for me because I still hadn't dealt with it. I was still very angry, upset, and hurt and I was still really missing him. I wasn't coping with it.

Mum didn't understand how I was feeling because she was dealing with it in her own way. Her faith in God helped her through, and if my faith had been as strong as hers, I'm sure it would have helped me too. My faith just wasn't that strong, and I was still angry with God.

My body became my enemy; and it was this attitude that got me through my workouts. At work I tried to continue as best I could, though my friends noticed the change in my weight. I could tell that I was losing weight by my clothes, but I just couldn't physically see any difference when I looked in the mirror; all I could see was an obese person staring back at me. At times I got really frustrated with my friends when they talked about my diet, for I was struggling to reach my next target weight of 7 stones. This made me very upset and angry with myself, so I decided to spend more time exercising. I made exercising fit into everything that I did. I would go for long walks in the afternoon on the weekends after gym, and would run up and down the stairs at home 10 times. I only did this on the weekends, while mum was at church, so she never saw what I was doing. I even went as far as using laxatives, I'm not sure why; I just decided to buy them one day and thought that they would help me to lose weight.

I guess I must have lost more weight, but I wasn't sure because I hadn't checked my weight in a long time. The scales also became my enemy, because they didn't show the results I wanted. I hated the fear that my weight wouldn't go down, and I just couldn't handle the disappointment. My work friends and family members became concerned once more, and they talked about me going to the doctor again; I guess by now I was beginning to think that I did have a bit of a problem. But I refused to believe I had anorexia or even an eating disorder; I just thought I needed a bit of help. I agreed to go back to see the doctor again, and this time I had someone with me. The doctor I saw was more helpful and he listened to me. He weighed me, which I hated, and then he referred me to the local hospital and a community team. When he asked me about the anti-depressant tablets and how I was getting on with them, I told him that they had not made a difference. I just had to wait until my appointment with the community team came through; the doctor said that it would take time for the hospital appointment to be arranged.

I went away feeling a bit relieved because I had told the doctor as much as I could. I am not sure whether I did the right thing, but I still felt that I had to continue with losing weight by exercising because I felt that if I stopped I would put the weight back on and not be able to control it. The thought of that would frighten me too much, and I just couldn't handle it.

When the appointment came through with the community team I was very nervous about it. I saw a nurse I recognized because she had visited mum at home. So at least I saw a face that I was familiar with. She talked to me about what was happening, and how I felt, and I explained to her as best I could. She simply said that all I had to do was to wait for the hospital appointment to come through.

As I waited for my appointment I was still not totally convinced that I had an eating problem. I knew that I needed help, but I was not convinced that I needed hospital help, and I didn't think it was really serious.

22. Hospital Treatment

When my appointment came through from the hospital, I was just dreading it. On the day of the appointment, I found the hospital quite easily, and I soon found the out-patient department. The doctor I saw was quite young-looking and very easy to talk to. When I walked into the room, he said "Hello. My name is Mr Graham, and I am the consultant for eating disorders. Tell me a bit about yourself and the problems you are having."

I told him that I worked with children, enjoyed my job, and lived at home with my mum. My dad had died recently, however. When he asked me what I ate, I told him that I had a drink during the day, and had a meal before 6pm, usually of rice or chicken or sweetcorn. Yesterday I had eaten some chicken, but I wasn't too sure. Mr Graham listened to me and then advised me go on a six week programme involving eating disorder problems and similar issues. I was also put on a waiting list to see a therapist.

I was so relieved when the appointment had finished; I thought that at least I would see what the programme was like and whether it would make a difference. I was not sure how much of a problem I had and still was not convinced that I had an eating disorder. I would just have to wait and see what would happen. I told everyone what was going to happen at the hospital, and they were happy that I was getting the help I needed. At first I was bit worried about what my employer would say because I would have to take time out of work to do the programme. I spoke to my manager, who was fine about, so at least I didn't have to worry about that. All I had to do now was to wait for the programme to start and I didn't have to wait very long.

The programme took place on the Eating Disorder ward, in one of the side rooms; there were two therapists running the programme and there were 6 of us on it. The therapist went through the subject of "The effects of having an Eating Disorder", and we were given handouts on this subject. Most of the programme emphasized the amount of damage that could be caused by eating disorders, such as lack of periods and the fact that the body will just shut down; finding all this out really surprised me. At the end of the programme I had a chat with one of the therapists. I just wanted to talk to her about how I felt, and I also spoke about my dad and his illness, becoming really emotional when I was speaking. I don't know why, for I've never broken down or cried in front of anyone, seeing crying as a weakness, and I didn't want to see myself as a weak person. I was disappointed that I had broken down in front of her, and felt that she wasn't even listening to me. All she said, in a sarcastic tone was, "You are not a happy bunny, are you?" I just wondered why I had allowed myself to get so low. I also thought, "What does she know about anything anyway? I bet she doesn't have a clue".

The programme finished after six weeks, and I tried to break the diet and to have a better eating plan during the day, but it was something I struggled with because I was scared of gaining weight, and I became scared of food.

IS THIS RECOVERY?

23. Visiting Jamaica With My Mum

I didn't realise that my life very much revolved around diet, exercise, body shape and the scales. I don't know how or when or even why, but it just did. My mum and family were still the centre of my life, and I loved and cared about them so much. I knew my mum's health was not good, but there was something I knew she always wanted to do, and that was to go back to Jamaica to see her family and close friends. I was never that keen to go to Jamaica, because I never found it interesting, and I just never got excited about it, maybe because I remembered dad never talked about it and was never interested in going back there. When he was alive he always said he would never go back, and he never did.

Mum really wanted to go, however, so I booked a holiday. I was looking forward to seeing my aunties, uncles and especially my dad's brothers, but I was a bit worried about how mum would cope with the flight. The holiday began on 14 May 1999. The flight was good and they catered for my mum's need by providing a wheelchair, so she didn't have to do much walking. When we arrived at Jamaica airport my cousin Tony picked us up and drove us to my mum's sister's home. It was quite a long, hot journey from Kingston airport to St Elizabeth and it took 4 hours. As we pulled up on the drive, my aunts, (my mum's younger sisters) were waiting to welcome us. It was lovely to see them, and they greeted and hugged us warmly. My mum had not seen them for over 15 years, and they were so happy to see each other and they had so much to talk about, so I just sat in the house and listened to them catching up with each other.

I worried about being in Jamaica for three weeks because there would be no gym there, but I intended to walk a lot, though I was worried about the amount of food I would be eating. I was worried that I would put on a lot of weight while I was in Jamaica because I would not be able to restrict my intake of food as I normally did not eat after 6pm. In Jamaica, however, I would not have control over that, and I was really concerned.

On the first day of the holiday we were offered a big

breakfast, but I just had a drink with a Jamaican bun, that was all I wanted. My Aunty said, "Veronica what you want to eat?" I replied, "Nothing yet, thank you." Then she said, "No, man, come have someting to eat." Then my Aunty said to my mum, "what wrong wid her, why she won't eat anything?" My mum said, "That's how she stay, she won't eat a ting."I thought to myself, hello I'm still here. I can hear you talking about me. I knew that they didn't mean any harm - they were just concerned about me.

Throughout the day my aunties kept offering me food; I accepted it, though after a while it became too much for me. This happened throughout the holiday. While I was on holiday, I thought about how food and eating is a big part of our culture. I would say yes to some meals and drinks, but only take a small amount for I could see they were offended when I said no. They all found me really strange. I guess in Jamaica there is no one with an eating disorder who restricts their food intake and over-exercises. While I was there I realised that I did have a problem and needed support. I was never going to get the help from someone from my own background and culture because they would never understand.

I enjoyed my holiday in Jamaica, although it was really hard to cope without exercising. I was able to go for walks, but these were not long, for it was just too hot. One day when I went for a walk, I felt really ill because of the heat and the amount I sweated. Sometimes I did some sit-ups and leg exercises in the house, which was better than doing nothing. I just ate as little as I could because I didn't want to gain weight while I was away.

The main reason I went to Jamaica was for my mum. It was important to me that she enjoyed herself. Meeting my family was good, the weather was brilliant, the scenery was breath-taking, and there were beautiful trees. There was clear blue water and lovely clean sand, and I had a brilliant time swimming in the sea. Meeting my dad's brothers was amazing, for it was like seeing my dad again - all three of them looked just like him.

24. Back to Life

When we got back to England, it was back to normal again with the weather, work, and everyday chores; it was a bit of a letdown when you have had a big holiday like we had just had. Mum was a bit down; she didn't seem like her normal self, but I just thought that she may have had a bit of the holiday blues, so I didn't look into it too much.

My appointment with the therapist came through; it was a one-to-one session. I was really nervous because I didn't know what to expect from these sessions. The first session was more like a get-to-know-each-other session, and she talked about herself a little and I let her know how much of a problem this eating disorder had become and when it all started. I found the one-to-one session difficult because I couldn't express myself clearly enough, and I didn't know what to say. There were gaps in the sessions when I didn't say anything and she didn't say anything to me; I found this very difficult. I thought all this was a waste of time, because maybe I was not fully ready for the therapy. I just didn't open up as much as I should have done, but I continued to work with this therapist, and once I got to know her a bit, and did more one-to-one sessions, it became more comfortable.

While I was having therapy, I felt that things were still not getting better; I still continued to over- exercise, and I still wasn't happy with my weight. I was now gaining weight, so I changed my eating plan, and restricted myself even more. I now started to eat at 7pm so I had nothing to eat or drink all day until that time. I now started to go to the gym at 7:30am every morning, working with Rosie, my close friend. Rosie was someone I could talk to, we had good laughs, and both enjoyed going to the gym. I'm not sure how much Rosie understood about the problems I had, but she always tried to support me. I enjoyed going to the gym so much that I would go an hour before and after work. It was hard but I loved it.

25. Day Care

I felt that because I was on a treatment programme for eating disorders, and I was in therapy, I would soon make a full recovery or at least, be signed off the treatment. I felt that my family wanted to see changes; I was really struggling, even though I was getting help now. But I was still hurting and was sad because I had never grieved for dad. No one ever spoke about him or even remembered him- it was as if he never existed in the first place. I was so angry with everyone and everything, but I didn't find it easy to express these feelings to anyone. It was very hard now, because I started to have health problems, feeling weak, and I was starting to have time off work because I was never well, though I still kept going with the exercising and diet plans. I needed to have something that would take away the feelings I had inside.

I always thought that mum was my closest and best friend, because she was the only one that saw what was happening to me, putting up with all my mood swings and the bad days. We had arguments; I guess it's always your nearest and dearest that you take it out on. Although others would lose their patience with me, she never did. She would just ask me why I didn't go to church, saying that I couldn't live without God in my life. She would then go on to say that I couldn't live like this, and then she would go and cook a meal for me, in the hope that I would eat it and everything would be alright.

I continued to see my therapist every week and I had appointments to see a consultant every three months. My previous consultant had left and I was now seeing a new one, who was really nice and easy to talk to, so I felt more relaxed with him. He recommended more help for me in the form of day care, which would involve regulated meals at set times and more one-to-one therapy. I agreed to be there from 8:30am to 7:30pm.

On the first day of the day care, the taxi arrived at 7:30am to take me to the hospital. I was introduced to the nurse in charge, who asked me about my eating habits and exercising regime, and also what I expected to gain from this programme. I just found the whole day care programme too much. The first meal I saw looked scary, and it took me forever to eat it. I struggled through the first days in the day care unit, it was so hard - no exercising -

we had to eat all day, and I was being weighed regularly. I was sure that I was the heaviest person on the programme, but the other girls on the programme were nice and I was able to relate to them. I couldn't cope in the Centre for long, but I stayed there for six weeks, and then left. This became a regular pattern, but I did eventually work out why I was behaving like this. I could not cope with the routine; so much sitting, completing every meal, having drinks and snacks, but no exercise. Maybe I wasn't ready for daycare and so I left the programme.

26. Disappointment with Day Care

I was a bit disappointed with the way the day care went, for I had hoped that it would help me, and that I would come out of it totally cured of the eating disorder. I guess that it was just wishful thinking because nothing changed. I came out of day care wanting to restrict my dieting more, and I started to take laxatives again. I took about 12 pills a day. This made me feel even better because I felt that I was getting rid of the anger I felt about myself. I also started to eat at 8pm instead of 7pm, just wanting to punish myself. I didn't deserve to be anything, and I needed to feel hurt and pain inside.

My therapy session with my first therapist had now finished, and my consultant said I should see another therapist because it could take several attempts at therapy before it would work. He also told me that all therapists work differently, and I was on put a waiting list.

I still continued to enjoy my work, for I love working with children. Even though I enjoy my work, I was still taking a lot of time off, which became a concern to my employer who then referred me to the Occupational Health Department. I didn't think they would know how to help me either, but I went to see them and explained what was happening to me. I felt I had to expose myself to another person, and so had no control of anything. So I took more laxatives in the hope that I would gain control.

I had a very close relationship with my nephews and nieces, Sandra, June, Sean, Jane, and Tracey. Sean and Jane spent a lot of time at my house because the school they attended was nearby, so they would come in the morning and then again after school. They were the reasons why I wanted to get better because I loved them very much and I wanted to be a strong, positive person for them. I also wanted to be there for all my family. Mum was a strong person; I often looked at her and wondered where she got her strength from, even after all the illnesses she had had. I know how much she enjoyed having her grandchildren around, for Sean and Jane lifted that lonely, sad feeling that was in the house since dad died, and I couldn't wish for better nieces and nephews. They don't know how much they mean to me and my mum, because we both found losing someone who was a big part of our lives so hard. It made me feel confused, but they were our tower of strength during this difficult time.

27. New Treatment Therapist

My next appointment came through to begin therapy again. With this therapist it was a lot easier to open up right away. She said that she wanted to try cognitive therapy with me, which she explained. I was a bit nervous about this because I was not sure what this would involve, but I thought I would have nothing to lose so I might as well give it a go.

My work with the new therapist was going really well, for I opened up to her and felt really comfortable talking to her. These sessions went really well even though I did find it hard to change. The demand for using laxatives was increasing, and I was now using 20 pills a day, and I continued to exercise and not to eat until 8pm. My weight was not going down much, however; even though everyone around me thought I was losing weight, I didn't think I was. I was too scared to weigh myself, and couldn't even think about it. My therapist was concerned, so she started to talk about me going into hospital. I was a bit concerned also because I knew I had a problem and I needed help, but I wasn't sure if the hospital was the right place for me. I think that I have struggled with the thought that maybe I don't have an eating disorder; you only see a lot of white people with the problem, (I know that is a crazy thought) so I just thought I was in the wrong place – black people don't have this problem!

In my culture, mental health is something that you never speak about, something that has to be swept under the carpet, something that you should be ashamed of. This is what I grew up with, and I never understood why I thought like that. When I explained how I felt to my therapist, she listened to me, but I'm not sure if she really understood how I felt about going into hospital. She asked me about how I would feel if she came to visit my mum and other family members to discuss the problems that I was having with this illness. I thought that this was a good idea; I wasn't sure whether they would understand, but I was keen to give it a go.

When I told mum about what my therapist had said, and about me going to hospital, it really worried her. I could tell mum couldn't understand why I wouldn't just eat and stop all of this. It was hard for me to understand, so how could I expect my mum to understand any of this? I spoke to my Aunty and Uncle about the meeting and they were more than happy to come along, and when I spoke to my brother George he too said he would be happy to come. I took the day of the meeting off work. I was more concerned about what everyone else would say than what the therapist would say. My therapist started by explaining about eating disorders in general, trying to make it as easy as she could for everyone. The main thing my therapist said was that I should go into hospital, and everyone agreed with this, as they realised I needed help. After the meeting my therapist stayed for a cup of tea and a chat and then she left. I felt the meeting went quite well and that it may have given my family an insight into my problem.

I talked to my mum when everyone had left and asked her if she understood what had been said. She said she had, but looked a bit worried. I think the illness was hard for her to grasp. She was the one who had seen the most changes in me. I had gone from being a daughter she could cook any meal for, eating happily, and who never worried about her weight and size, never went to the gym, nor did any exercise, to someone who always worried about her weight and size. Since my dad had died, I suppose my mum had seen me give up on life because I also stopped going to church and that was very hard for her to understand. She had an awful lot to deal with already, because she was still missing my dad and although Sean and Jane came every day before and after school, she was usually alone during the day.

I was on the waiting list to go to hospital, but it was very hard because I was off work, and so had more time to go to the gym. I was taking more and more laxatives every day, feeling that I had to lose weight. I weighed myself when I went in, and I hated everyone knowing my weight, feeling so ashamed and even more disgusted with myself. I had to wait about a month before I got the phone call to say there was a bed for me at the hospital. I did have a chance to visit the unit, but there wasn't much to see- just the dining room, the living room and the counseling rooms where I had been when I was in day care. The bedrooms had eight beds which seemed small and cramped, two bathrooms, which eight patients had to share; there was a bathroom routine which I thought would be a nightmare in the mornings. There was a laundry where you could do your washing and ironing, and that was it. Marcia went to look around the unit when she was pregnant with Paul and quite close to her due date, and she thought it was quite nice. It was really good of her to come with me.

28. Hospital Admission

The day came for me to go in. I was scared, but I knew I would come out better, and over this horrible, frustrating lonely and painful illness. The morning I went into hospital I received the fantastic news that I had another nephew, Paul. I was worried, however, because I didn't know when I would get a chance to see him. I was hoping that I wouldn't be in hospital for long. When I arrived, the nurses did a bag search. I couldn't understand why they needed to do that, but as soon as they found my laxatives I knew why they searched patients' bags. I guess that because I was taking so many laxatives every day I was becoming dependent on them, and I thought I couldn't manage without them.

I was later seen by a doctor who asked a lot of questions about the history of my eating disorder, when it started and how it affected my daily life. The doctor also gave me a physical examination; he checked my blood pressure, did a chest check and checked my weight, which of course I hated. I then went onto the ward to settle in, and I was introduced to the other patients, who all seemed very nice. I selected my bed and unpacked.

It took me a few days to settle in. I still believed that I didn't need to be there especially since all the other patients were thinner than me, so I felt more uncomfortable around them, and even more so when we talked about the body mass index. I felt so fat among them; there were days when I would really struggle, particularly during meal times; I wasn't able to complete most meals. Meal times always seemed to last an eternity; and I hated the drinks. All they had was tea and coffee as hot drinks (which I don't like) or for cold drinks orange or blackcurrant squash (which they always made too watered down).You were made to finish every meal and all your drinks, which amounted to a lot of pressure and often I would be in tears. I was blocking out all my emotions by not eating, by taking excessive exercise, and by taking laxatives. So by being in the hospital, where they took all this away from me, life was very difficult. It seemed that all you did in hospital was to eat; we would have sitting times one hour after dinner and also half an hour after a drink. I felt that I needed more counselling, but although the nurses were all very nice, I needed to feel really comfortable before I could truly open up to anyone.

I had a lot of visitors while I was in hospital, but it was hard to talk about how everything was going with my treatment, and I could see that friends and family still couldn't understand my illness. I remember a question that one of my visitors asked when they came to see me: "If you can eat here at the hospital, how come you can't eat at home?" I thought it was a stupid question to ask. Mum came up most days, and it was lovely to see her. Sometimes she would struggle to get to the hospital, and on the days she couldn't make it she would always phone to see how I was; that was a good thing about mum, we sometimes had our disagreements and had some bad times, but I knew she would always be there for me supporting me, and I would do the same for her.

I struggled with the fact that I had to be weighed twice a week in hospital; my weight kept on going up all the time, and this scared me, making me wish that I wasn't there. I believed that the most important thing in life was my weight and what the scales were telling me. This was what most of the patients talked about, and most of them worried about meal times also.

I stayed in hospital for a month and when I was discharged, I couldn't wait to go home. I was on edge, because I couldn't wait to get back to my exercising. There was a mini gym in the hospital, but I was restricted in the time I was allowed to use it. I felt that the hospital didn't tackle any of the issues that I needed it to. I was released from hospital and returned home, but I didn't go back to work straightaway. I realise now that that was a bad idea, because I just slipped back into my old routine of laxatives, exercise, and restrictive eating regimes. I just felt fat, and thought that I needed to lose weight.

When I returned home I continued with the exercising, restrictive eating habits and the laxative abuse, not because I wanted to. I tried to stop; I tried eating small amounts during the day but always at the back of my mind something reminded me that I shouldn't be eating because I was Fat and I needed to lose weight. These thoughts became unbearable, and made eating, which should be an enjoyable thing, seem like a nightmare. While I was at hospital, I started to think about renewing my faith and returning to church; people from church were so supportive of me whilst I was in hospital even though they didn't fully understand my problem. I didn't return fully to church; I went on the odd occasion, but I don't think it helped me much.

I thought that by going into hospital, I would be totally cured, and it was so frustrating to see that the problem was still there. I didn't know what else to do, so slipping back into my old routine seemed like the easiest option. I couldn't deal with my thoughts about my body shape; I hated eating, but I loved exercising. The lack of change upset my mum, who thought that she would have seen improvements in me. This made matters worse, and I avoided meal times with her.

When I returned to work, I tried my hardest to eat by bringing my own packed lunch, but the moment anyone commented on what I was eating, I would panic. I couldn't cope with eating meals around others, especially at work, so I stopped eating at work. This made me think I was doing the right thing, and I felt comfortable and really happy.

29. Home Again

Life returned to normal, and I made up for lost time with my nieces and nephews especially Paul, who was born the day I was admitted to hospital; I gave him lots of cuddles. I decided that it would be nice for me and mum to go away for a while at a church conference held in Brighton, so we booked up for 5 days in a really nice hotel near the conference hall, which was excellent for mum. It was nice for mum to have a break; she could sit back and relax not having to worry about a thing. Mum enjoyed the conference, which finished far too soon for our liking, but it was nice for us to get away. I personally liked the conference for it made me think a lot about God and my own faith. At times I would wish that I could be normal and go back to how I was before all this started.

I continued to see my therapist at the hospital, but I felt I was still unable to make changes in my life, which was very annoying. I couldn't eat regularly; I found it hard to stop what I was doing, and I could see that my therapist was getting a little frustrated too. She worked so hard on me and had even arranged to do a talk at my local church; she did this later, though I'm not sure how much the church members took in and understood. I was grateful for her attempts, but I knew that in our culture we tend to dismiss these problems.

One year after my admission into hospital, and nothing had changed, for I still had problems and I was sinking deeper and deeper. Work was getting harder because I took so much time off; I was still seeing the therapist, but I couldn't see any changes, and became more frustrated and unhappy. I knew that I had become unhappy when dad became ill, and I felt that a part of me was buried with him. This is probably why I couldn't change or even see any light at the end of the tunnel. I never told anyone how I was feeling. I know that we will all die one day, but I believe it is important to talk about dying and losing loved ones, and it's just not on to say that the person is better off or is in a better place. My faith wasn't strong enough to accept that idea and a comment like that just made me angry.

I wanted to find myself again, but I felt that I couldn't. I decided to go to Canada to visit my cousin Amanda at the end of April. When I wrote to her, she replied that she was more than happy for me to come over. So I booked the holiday and flew over, having warned her about my eating habits before I went. I loved it there - the weather was lovely, and Canada was just a great place to be. I felt so relaxed and happy there, although I missed mum a lot, and hoped she'd be alright at home.

I stayed in Montreal, in the French-speaking side of Canada. The houses were big and pretty. Amanda had two cute children, I loved their Canadian accents, and I was able to make myself feel at home. Amanda told me about the local bus services and tubes, but for the first couple of days she took me out and told me how to get around. I went to all the tourist areas and enjoyed visiting the sites of Canada; I also loved the shops and the underground shopping. It was all fantastic.

While I was there Amanda made the mistake of taking me to the local gym which she was going to join. That was it. I went there every other day, the walk taking about 20 minutes; I would spend 1½ hours there, then walk back to Amanda's. I did a lot of walking, and didn't mind at all because the weather was great. I was really enjoying myself, and I loved it there, so I was so disappointed when the holiday came to an end. Amanda was so lovely, and we really did get on well - I had a fantastic time. I liked Canada so much that I would love to live there.

I didn't want to come back from Canada, although I missed everyone at home, especially my family. It was lovely seeing mum again; she had been fine without me, and told me that church people had been phoning her constantly to check she was alright, and our neighbours and uncle had also popped in from time to time. It was hard after a holiday like that to be able to slip back into normal life again, because I was on so much of a high about Canada. When friends asked if I would live out there, I said "tomorrow, if I could." They were all so happy that I had had such a good time; however, my eating problem still existed and I still had that empty feeling inside.

After returning from my holiday I started to attend a support group, which was held at the hospital for people who have an eating disorder. We talked about any difficulties and struggles we had in day-to-day life around the eating disorder. Going to the support group and listening to everyone made it clear that I did have a problem and that others were struggling with this too. I talked about the problems and the struggles that I had had in Canada, and the group just listened and offered me advice for future holidays.

I had had to do without laxatives while I was away, so I just cut back on them now and I stopped depending on them. I therefore avoided the stomach cramps that they caused, and since they didn't help with weight loss it was just a waste of money. I was still doing two workouts a day, and I was not eating anything until 8pm. I did lose some weight while I was away, but I didn't think that I had lost any.

THOUGHTS AND EMOTIONS

30. Mum's Relapse

I noticed a change with my mum, because she started to say things that didn't make sense or were not correct. When I spoke to her Community Nurse, she said she would call round to see her and monitor how she was, and just keep an eye on her. But mum was just getting more and more confused; she went up and down the stairs all night, and opened the front door in the middle of the night. I just wished that I could help her but I didn't know what to do to help. When she became ill there was nothing I could say, and it was difficult leaving her because she was on her own. Sean and Jane couldn't come because she was too ill. I found that all I was doing was ringing everyone to let them know, and they would come round and ask mum to take her tablets. But she was too confused to know and this continued for two weeks, until the local mental health team decided that mum needed to go into hospital. However, Mum refused to go, so the next stage was to have her sectioned which was the last thing I wanted to happen to her. But I couldn't convince her to go into hospital. George and Mark and everyone else tried too, but she wouldn't listen, and so had to be sectioned under the Mental Health Act Section 3. The ambulance and the police came and she went with them; I went with her, even though she thought that I was against her too.

The next day, when I went to see her she didn't want to talk to me, she was so ill. I wished that I could understand mum's illness, for I would have been able to respond quicker, and all these community health people wouldn't have to get involved. This is what makes me feel so cross about things. I feel that as a community we should not brush things under the carpet, but try to find out about conditions, both physical and, mental. I was never told when I was growing up, so I just didn't know how to help her, and it was so hard and upsetting to watch her getting so ill without being able to help. I just felt so guilty and useless, feeling that it was my fault that mum had become so ill. I now know that it would take a while for mum to get better.

I visited mum every day. She was quite ill, especially in

the first week, being confused and unsettled. I rang the ward every day; sometimes they would say that she was still very unsettled and I just kept on thinking how long it would take. I also wondered if I might have seen more signs that things were not right, but I have never really understood schizophrenia because it had never been explained to me. I thought that the community team might have thought that we all knew what it was, and that we were able to spot the signs. They may have been surprised when I didn't ask them for information and advice.

It took mum about 7-10 days to settle down in the hospital. She was happy for me and George and Mark and family and church friends to visit. The nurses said that it would take a while, and that once she had begun to respond to treatment she would be easier to visit. They also told me that because she was so unwell I should not worry about what she said to me. I did take on board what they said to me, but I was still very upset to see her so ill and confused. The next few weeks mum became more and more settled, more herself again, and happy to see me. She spent two months in hospital, and just before she was discharged there was a Discharge Care Plan meeting which both me and mum attended. Mum's consultant asked me a lot of questions about me and my problems, which was hard for me especially when to my surprise I found 7 professional people around the table- social workers, home helpers, nurses, community nurses and others. I managed to say as much as I could although I felt uncomfortable, mainly because mum's consultant and my consultant were keeping in touch about both of us. By the end of the meeting it was decided that mum would have home care visits - one in the morning to help her with breakfast, and a second at night. They would also visit the house to see if she needed any more help around the house with equipment. Mum was happy with everything, and with the help that she was going to get. I was so happy to see her so well, back to the mum I knew and loved so much; happy and smiling, talking, sharing her love for God, and telling me how important it was to have him in my life, encouraging others as well. It had taken a lot out of me to see mum so ill, and I just wanted to focus all my time on her and to concentrate and see her get better. My own illness was the last thing on my mind.

31. Mum's Discharge

The day came for mum to be discharged. It was so good to see her well again and back at home, and she was really happy to be home again. While she was in hospital we had had a new toilet built for her so that she didn't have to keep walking up and down the stairs. The home carers came in the morning to help her to dress and make her breakfast, and they also came in the evening to help her into bed. I didn't feel that they were really necessary, but it was a bit of extra support for mum. Because of everything that was going on with mum I was not coping at work; I was not dealing with my eating disorder so I was just going downhill, and I was also really upset. When I was told by my therapist that her work with me had to come to an end because a therapist can only work with a patient for two years, I was really dissapointed. I had become really close to her and responded really well to her. I sent her a card to say thank you for everything, so I could get closure on our work together and try to move on.

While I was off work I tried really hard to change my eating pattern during the day. But I constantly had battles with this - why was I eating? I shouldn't be eating during the day, it was not right. I also got really worried that I was gaining a lot of weight which was just making me freak out. I needed to try to change, because I wanted to show the so-called experts that I could indeed change and that I did want to help myself. Part of me was angry with the hospital and my ex-therapist and I just thought that I really had to try to change because I didn't want to live the rest of my life like this. Every day when I tried to eat something during the day or have a drink it was one big battle.

32. My Diary Entries

I started to record my thoughts in a diary during this difficult time. On 14th May 2002 I wrote, *"I still felt really big and overweight, I wish I could change the way I am. I ate half an apple, with a drink and bits of a bread roll; then I went to a body pump class today. I really enjoyed the really hard work, and I am trying to cope with exercise and eating normally". I have to do this for myself"*. One month later on 19th June 2003 I wrote, *"Today is going to be a hard day, I feel so down and I just feel like giving up. Sometimes it just seems so hopeless, and I will never make a full recovery. I suppose I just have to take one day at a time. I managed to have a snack bar and a drink today. I went to the support group, it was alright. I suppose it helps to talk"*. I realised that this illness wasn't going to go away unless I was willing to try really hard, and I would have to continue to work at it every day. I was trying really hard to make small changes, but I was off work, and my mum had just returned home with physical as well as mental illness and it was tough for both of us. There were times when we would both have a bad day and we could take it out on each other, but I knew that my mum was still my tower of strength, although I always knew that her answer would be that she would pray for me, and that I really should go back to church. By her saying that, and hearing my mum pray for me, meant the world to me because I know that God is the reason why I still have a chance to be here and a chance to change.

There was a new female doctor at the surgery and she was brilliant. I always found it really easy to talk to her, for she always listened to me, and the good thing about her was that she always talked about God and my faith, and she helped me because she was willing to do a report about my current health to the Occupational Health worker - which would hopefully help with my return to work. Anyway, I wanted to be the one who was going to show that this was an illness that you can change and that it is an illness that anyone can have. When I had my interview with the Occupational Health worker I talked about my problems and she was happy for me to return to work. She asked me to come every two weeks so that she could keep an eye on things and see how I was getting on. My eating and drinking were beginning to slip again; perhaps I was trying to do too much for mum, as well as worrying about work. I had started to apply for jobs because I was thinking that a fresh start would be better for me, and I was also trying hard to develop an eating plan during the day on those days when it was a real struggle. When I wrote in my diary on 27th July 2002 that I was feeling a bit down, I think it was because I had realised that I had a long uphill struggle and would have to live with the illness. I suppose realising that had made me feel down, because I wanted recovery tomorrow morning but that was not going to happen. I had a nice quiet day thinking about all these things.

I managed to keep myself going by focusing on mum, on my nieces, and my nephews Sean, Jane and Paul. They were one of the reasons why I could never give up on myself. My brother George would often visit us, and encouraged me to be positive. George used to be in a running club, so he knew a lot about fitness and how to look after one's body. He would often say that I could really damage my body by exercising on nothing; I listened, but because nothing bad ever happened I thought it would never happen to me. I felt that I could share things with George for he was easy to talk to. I would chat over the phone with Rosie, and we went to the cinema together and I would go round to see her house for a chat and a laugh. I also had a very close church friend called Pam who used to ring me up and just have a girly chat. They both said I was doing really well especially with mum, though I worried about mum's health. I wrote in my diary on 2nd August 2002. *"I went to the gym in the morning then I came back to take mum to get her eyes tested. It scared me, how slow she has become, and how much of her self-help skills she has lost. It's really hard to watch her the way she is at the moment, and it's not going to get any better. It is going to get harder. Watching her reminds of dad and how he became before he got really ill and died. I wonder if the same thing will happen. I don't know, it really scares me. I didn't manage to eat anything during the day today. It seems so hard at the moment."*

It was just at this time that mum had another fall. On 6th August 2002. I wrote in the diary. *"What a day; mum had a fall this morning so I had to ring for an ambulance for her. She had to go to hospital, and the doctor told me she might have broken her hip. I nearly died, I was so shocked. She was admitted to the ward this afternoon. It has just been an awful year for her. I am just so fed up at the moment. I didn't manage to eat anything during the day today."* The next day, when I visited mum in hospital, the doctor said she may have just bruised her hip, which was what the x-ray showed. The next few days I had to keep hoping for the best, and it started to look hopeful because they managed to get mum back on her feet. She had managed to walk a very short distance on the ward with help from the nurses. I was beginning to get stressed and anxious, because I would be returning to work in a few weeks, and because I had been off for such a long time.

I was really missing my therapist because we worked very well together. But sooner or later these sessions would have ended and I would have had to manage on my own. I still saw her in the support group, however, because she was one of the leaders. I continued to attend that group and found it very useful. Listening to people who have the same illness gave me the will to keep fighting the illness, and I could also give others advice and hope.

I started back at work full-time. It was always difficult to bring drink and food into work because I worried about eating and drinking in front of everyone, thinking that they saw me as a greedy fat cow. All these thoughts were going on in my head most of the time, and I was convinced that everyone else thought the same way too. I did manage to have a drink on my own, however. My return to work was going alright apart from the fact that I was still struggling with my eating and drinking. My friends supported me as much as they could, and Rosie and I continued to do a lot outside of work. We both really loved tennis and went to the Davis Cup tournament. I wrote in my diary 21st September 2002, *"I had a really good day today. I went to the Davis Cup tournament with Rosie and really enjoyed myself. It was nice to do something with Rosie again. We did a bit of window-shopping in town, and then we stopped for a drink of white wine with lemonade. I drank some of it. The tennis was really good."* So I had had a brilliant day and I didn't go to the gym, but because I was busy all day I didn't mind it too much. Rosie and I would also watch Wimbledon, phoning and texting each other to comment on how Tim Henman was playing (I think Rosie had a bit of a soft spot for him). We also had tennis lessons together. One week after the Davis Cup match a few friends organised a night out, though I was not sure whether to go or not. I wrote in my diary, *"I am supposed to be going out tonight with Rosie, Catherine and Stacey, I want to go but I'm not sure about it, night clubs are not my scene. In fact I went to the gym, I visited mum in hospital and then decided to go. It was a wild night out, but it was good fun we had a laugh and we let our hair down. I didn't manage to eat anything during the day but I did manage to have a drink while I was out and I'm glad I went".*

The next few days would be difficult because mum was about to be discharged. They had done a lot of work with her in hospital to get her back on her feet, particularly with the way she got in and out of bed. She did well on some days, but not on others. The discharge date was set and mum was discharged. When she came back home it was hard for her in the early days as she needed time to adapt at home. I felt she just wasn't coping, and it was suggested that mum should move her bedroom downstairs. So the front room had to be sorted out for her. She had a good social worker and an Occupational Therapist who was really nice, for it was easy to approach her about anything. There was a church friend who would pop round during the day when I was at work. They would cook for mum and go shopping. But the most important thing that needed to be sorted out was the front room, and this was done by me and the social worker. A bed came from the hospital, so mum could move in downstairs straightaway, and we waited to see how that would work out for her. My plan to bring some order into my eating went out of the window, but I was pleased with myself because I really gave it a go. I wrote down all my feelings and thoughts in my diary, which helped me to deal with things and get some of my anger and frustration down instead of taking it out on myself. I just had to keep working on my eating and take it one day at a time.

It was going to be hard at work because Rosie had got another job and would soon be leaving, which was very sad news for me, although I was really pleased for her, because she really was looking forward to a new start. A leaving party was organised for her, but I was not sure about it. I wanted to go because Rosie had been a really good friend, so I went to the meal; I didn't eat anything because I arrived late. But I was glad I went. I stayed in touch with Rosie, though, meeting her at kick aerobics class on a Thursday evening. I was glad that Rosie was really happy in her new job. Although it was really strange at work now that she was not there, I got on with the other girls; but it just was not the same. I had a good relationship with Rosie and I really did miss that.

Mum was settling down more at home now that her bedroom was downstairs and she got a lot of support from church members who arranged a meeting at home for her. I wrote in my diary on 25th November 2002 *"We had a prayer meeting last night when people talked about dad and mum, and what good people they are. I found it comforting and it was nice to hear people talk about dad."* I found this meeting very emotional. It was good hearing my dad being mentioned, and also mum, who was not able to go to church because she was so unstable on her feet; but at least all her hard work and prayer was still being recognized (although of course the hard work you do as a Christian can only be truly rewarded by God and by him alone). When he calls us home I do truly believe we will go to him. Although I am struggling with my Christian faith, and feel I will for a long time, George was really encouraging me to come to church with him and I said I would one day, and I left it like that.

Everything was going alright at home and at work, but then mum had another accident. I wrote in my diary on 5th December 2002, *"I had a better day at work today. I had a "performance management" session at work with one of my managers, which actually went well. She made me think about the future at work and the things that I wanted to do to improve myself. When I arrived home I found mum on the floor. It was really scary. She had to go to the hospital, where they thought she just had a water infection, but when the nurses tried to get her to walk she could not move her right leg. I thought she might have had a stroke, which scared me even more. I asked mum when she had fallen, and she said that it had been earlier in the afternoon, so she had been lying on her own for at least 2-3 hours on the cold kitchen floor. I just couldn't understand why mum was having so many falls. The next day I went to see mum, nothing had changed; over the next few days nothing changed, she was unable to walk".*

I couldn't work out why mums leg was just giving up on

her all the time and the doctors didn't really say anything, so it was a mystery. Mum would have to spend that Christmas in hospital, for there was no hope that she would be able to come home - this would be a Christmas with no family get-together, which was really strange. Normally Christmas is busy; mum always baked about 4 cakes, did a lot of shopping, made sure all her nieces and nephews and their children got a card and present. Mum always made sure that her family in Jamaica received gifts too. I made sure that presents still went out, because although mum was not able to do it, I still wanted her family, her sons and especially her grandchildren to know that mum still loved them even though they knew she couldn't do much now. On Christmas day, 25th December 2002, I wrote in my diary, *"Christmas Day. I had a good day today though it was difficult at times. I had a phone call from the hospital to say that mum had had a fall, but she was alright. When I visited her she seemed, down, but she had a lot of visitors today which made her a bit happier. I went to visit uncle in the morning then to Mark's, and finally to George's in the evening so I had quite a good day."*

Mum began to feel brighter and better in herself over the Christmas period. I visited her every day and I spent most of the Christmas holiday with her. She had a lot of visitors over Christmas and the New Year. On the last day of the year I didn't go out, but saw the New Year in on my own. I wrote in my diary on the 31st December 2002, *"I am so glad that it is the last day of the year, for this has been a really bad year. I sat up and I was happy to see 2003 in hopefully things will be better for me and mum this year. So it is a brand new year and I am hoping for a more successful and happy New Year, taking one day at a time."*

I was looking forward to returning to work after the Christmas break. When I returned to work I still visited mum every day, but her progress was really slow. One evening while I was visiting I was told that the consultant wanted to see me, so an appointment was made. Mum got really upset with me on my visits and we just ended up arguing, taking our anger out on each other. Mum wasn't going to argue with her sons, her brothers or anyone else; it was always the closest and the dearest, which was me, and I took all my frustrations out on her. But whatever happened or was said when we argued, she was still my mum and I loved her. My uncle and my auntie would ring and encourage me, saying that I shouldn't take it too seriously or let it get to me.

33. Diary Entries 2003

I went to the meeting with mum's consultant and I wrote in my diary on 16th January 2003, *"I had the meeting with the consultant (mum's) who said that mum would be severely disabled. He feels that she would be better off in a nursing home, which is a bit of a shock. I don't know what and where to go from here really."* I didn't manage to eat anything during the day. The next day one of the Occupational Therapists came to visit our home to see what could be done. I wrote in my diary on 17th January 2003. *"I went into work late today because the Occupational Therapist from the hospital came to look at the house to see what they could do; she was also very worried about mum returning home. I will try to talk to mum about it all later. I didn't manage to eat anything today. The hospital continues to show a lot of concern about mum, and whether it would be a good idea for her returning home."*

I wrote in my diary on 20th January 2003. *"I had an ok day at work today. I went to see mum, who doesn't seem to be getting any better. The nurses were saying how hard it would be when mum comes home, and that they didn't think that I would cope with her. I don't know what to do. I didn't manage to eat anything today."*

I just didn't know what quality of life she would have, stuck in the front room all day with nobody around. I would be at work, and she would never get out of the house because the front steps were too high, and nobody would have come to help her. I didn't want that for my mum for she deserved better, and I knew that mum didn't want to go in a nursing home, so I spoke to George to get his advice. I even spoke to Dr Barnes too because I was now so upset by the whole thing and it was affecting me at work. I started to see another therapist, but I only had about three sessions and then had to stop working with him because there was just too much going on at the time. The social worker and the hospital staff started to put together a package for mum to return because that's what she wanted. I said I would give it a go because I could see that mum was getting really stressed and upset about it. I found it really hard because the social worker would ring me and say that she had a package plan together, and then the next week she would ring me back and say it had been turned down. This all affected my work and my friendship with my close friends.

It was coming up to the anniversary of dad's death, and although it had been a while now I was still missing him a lot. I wrote in my diary on the 14th February 2003. *"Its 8 years since dad died; so much has happened, some good things also so many bad things. How I wish that he was still here with us, laughing and joking, watching all the sports on Sky, and giving me advice. I didn't manage to eat anything today. I am still really missing dad. He was the centre of our family and he would have been here for mum and me - nothing was a problem to him."*

The problems with mum coming home continued. I wrote in my diary on 19th February, *"I had an ok day today, doing the usual things. When I visited mum, she was in a right state because her social worker had told her that the grant for her home help package had been turned down, so she was very unhappy. I don't know what to do anymore. I didn't manage to eat anything during the day."* It was really getting hard, for mum was getting more and more worked up, angry and upset. But no one likes to be told that they cannot live in their own house (there's no place like home.)". I wrote in my diary on 23rd February, *"I had a quiet day, but I worried all day about mum, and the future. When I went to visit her today, she was crying. When she saw Sean and Jane she was equally upset and I just don't know what to say to mum any more"*.

Mum certainly needed care and support now because she was in a wheelchair, having lost the use of her legs. Someone needed to be there for her 24 hours a day. I wouldn't feel happy going to work, knowing that she would be at home for most of the day on her own. She might try to reach for something and fall out of the chair or the bed, and I didn't want to come home to find her on the floor again. I wrote in my diary on the 8th March 2003, *"I had a good day today. I took Sean out as a special treat for passing his 11+ exam, I am so proud of him. We went to see "Catch me if you can" at the cinema, and Jane came too. I did manage to have a drink today. I am so happy for Sean who is very clever and works hard even though he is quite young: I can see him going on to University. This is really good news for the family, because sometimes it seems all negative, so Sean going off to grammar school is great news, and well worth celebrating."* When I went to visit mum, today, 9th March 2003, I wrote in my diary, *"I had an ok day today I cleaned the house, ironed, went to the gym, and visited mum. She seems to be hearing voices again and also seems to be very distant too. I don't know, the whole situation's just one big mess."*

I wrote in my diary on the 26th March, *"I had a good day. I heard that mum would be coming home, but I was scared and left feeling very worried about how things would work out when she comes home. I'll just have to wait and see. I went to the support group which was ok. I didn't manage to eat anything during the day. I thought that mum was getting very unsettled but I couldn't work out why. It's Mother's Day and all of us visited mum today. George came to visit her, and it was really sad for mum because she is getting so ill and because she has spent so much time in hospital. I don't know how to help mum. I just feel so hopeless to be just watching her; I just wish that I could do something."*

The Occupational Therapist from the hospital came to the house to set up all mum's equipment; she brought a hoist and a special hospital bed with sides and a special chair and a tray. They also set up the room the best way they could for mum. I also had a chat with Stella at work about her, for I felt that it was important that they knew what was happening. I was pleased that everything was moving in the right direction and I wrote in my diary on 6th April 2003: *"I didn't do much today. I visited the gym and I also visited mum, who may be coming out on Wednesday if she gets a bit better, but she seems very confused and angry. I didn't manage to eat anything today."*

The next day I wrote, *"I had an ok day today, though I feel really tired. The days are so busy and long with work and hospital visits. Mum was a bit irritable and unsettled again today, and I feel a bit angry with the staff on the ward because I feel that they have ignored mum. They have not picked up on her illness. I didn't manage to eat anything today."* I felt that mum was in a hospital – yes, but it wasn't a hospital that dealt with mental health problems; they just seemed to be totally unaware of her needs. They were always so busy, but hopefully somebody would pick up on it. On 11th April: *"I had an ok day today. I didn't manage to go to the support group today. I visited mum; she is going to be seen by the hospital psychiatrist before she can come home. I didn't manage to eat anything during the day."* I was glad, because I didn't want her to come home where it might all go wrong. On the 12th April 2003: *"I have been so tired today and am so glad it's Friday. I just want to relax for a few days. Mum was seen today by the hospital psychiatrist. The hospital contacted me at 9:00am this morning while I was at work, but I couldn't get out to be there. They did think that mum was ill and they were going to move her to the Q.E.P. Hospital on Monday. I am feeling really down about this, I didn't manage to eat anything during the day."* At least I knew that mum was being sorted out now and hopefully she would be home soon. When mum was moved to the Q.E.P.H I visited her and wrote in my diary on the 14th April 2003: *"I had an ok day at work today. Mum was moved over to the Q.E.P.H today. When I visited her she was very sleepy so I didn't stay for long. I didn't manage to eat anything today."* It took a few days for mum to settle down in the hospital, though the staff knew her very well and were really nice and friendly. I wasn't sure what was going to happen. I still didn't know whether mum would be coming home or whether she would be going into a nursing home. Everything was on hold at the moment, which was good; at least I didn't have to worry so much about it for a while.

I planned a day out to Stratford-upon-Avon with a couple of the girls who attended the support group and had arranged this day out. I wrote in my diary on the 25th April 2003: *"I went to Stratford-upon- Avon with Susan, Claire and Linda. I was a bit quiet at first because I felt a bit uncomfortable, but I became more relaxed as the time went on. I enjoyed myself, and the day went quite well".* The only thing that made me feel disappointed about the day was that we stopped for a drink at a cafe in Stratford-upon-Avon, but I found it hard to have a drink with them. I was a bit annoyed with myself for this. I found it difficult to eat and drink with anyone, because I see eating and drinking as a social thing, and it's so hard to use food as a social thing to do.

My appointments with my consultant continued, although I didn't feel that I was getting anywhere. I wrote in my diary on 12th May 2003:*"I had an appointment at the hospital with my consultant, even though it seems to be just a waste of time. Someone is meant to tell me how to deal or stop doing so much exercising, but that will be a waste of time just like everything else I have tried to do in the last 2 years or so. I had an ok day at work. I didn't manage to eat anything during the day. I just find it all so pointless, maybe because I am struggling so much at the moment."* I wrote in my diary 21st May 2003. *"I had a good day at work. I felt that I did more with the children and the day didn't seem so long. I went to the support group today, but I was so fed up with it that I walked out half way through, when they started to talk about being in the Brownies. I don't think that I can keep going to that hospital for much longer, since I am not getting anything from it and I feel that I have failed with all the treatment that I have had. It all seems hopeless and pointless. I didn't manage to eat anything during the day."*

I wrote in my diary on 23rd May 2003. *"It was a staff training day today; it was good, better than I expected it to be. I also spoke to mum's social worker - not good news, but then it never is. When I visited mum she just seems really down; it's so sad to see her like that. I didn't manage to eat anything during the day."* The next day I had a very busy day and that helped me to take my mind off things. On 24th May 2003: *"I had a busy day today I had my hair done, and I also brought Fiona with me have her hair plaited too. I managed to fit the gym in. The day ended with me and Kirsty visiting mum, who is much better today. I went to Kirsty's house and enjoyed being with people all day - that makes a big difference to me and my moods, and helps to take my mind off things. I didn't manage to eat anything during the day."* I was beginning to realise that being on my own was not a good idea, for my head was filled with negative thoughts about my body, my shape, and my weight. I also thought about the situation with mum, and it was at these times that I really missed dad being around. I also found that when things got too much it was better to get away for a break, so I was really looking forward to this break. Everyone told me that Greece was lovely, with lots of things to see and do.

It wasn't long to my holiday; I was getting my clothes together, and it was good fun going shopping with Catherine and Stacey. They were a laugh, and I had a great time when I was with them.

At last things with mum were now a lot better; she had settled down on the ward and was not so confused. A case conference was set up which involved a social worker, her consultant and a nurse from the ward. I wrote in my diary on the

9th June 2003: *"A good day at work today. I am trying to get all my reports done before I finish for my holiday. At the case conference for mum they told me that mum wouldn't be able to return home again, which I suppose is for the best. We will have to talk to mum about it. I didn't manage to eat anything during the day."* I was nervous about talking to mum about the future, for I wasn't sure how she would take it, though I thought she was starting to accept the fact that being at home would be very hard. I also think that the care she would have received wouldn't have been very good, because someone would have had to be there for 24 hours every day of the week. If I had been at home it would have needed me and two other people to help lift her in and out of the bed, and she wouldn't get that from Care in the Community. I was told that it would cost less to have mum in a nursing home. This was hard to accept of course, and I felt that I had failed mum. I wrote in my diary on the 15th June 2003, *"I was very busy today, I went to the grave because it was Father's Day today and because I have not been for so long. I wrote a Father's Day card and collected my tickets in town; I met Catherine and went back to her house. I managed to have a drink there too; mum has accepted that she will have to go into a nursing home, which is good."* Diary 16th June 2003. *"I go on holiday tomorrow. I am so nervous about it as I'm not sure if I have done the right thing. I am sure I will be alright once I get there. I had a good morning at work and finished at dinner time. I went to the gym, then collected Paul from nursery and visited mum."* I was looking forward to my holiday, but I always felt so guilty when I left mum. At least I knew that she was being looked after, and I knew I could ring the hospital every day. If anything happened the family was there and I could get back to Birmingham if necessary. I needed to go in order to relax for a week.

I loved it in Greece, or rather, the island of Cephallonia. I had seen the film of "Captain Corelli's Mandolin" and it was brilliant to see the places where the film was made, and to look down on the beach where the big mine was exploded. I went shopping every day, and did a lot of sightseeing even though it was very hot, which I find very hard because I don't drink very much during the day, and because I do so much walking. I also tried to eat as little as I could because I was so scared that I would put on a lot of weight without going to the gym. I met some lovely people when I was sightseeing, and we even took each other's phone numbers. I was so sorry when my holiday came to an end, for I had had a fantastic time. I enjoyed it in Greece and would love to go again. I really enjoy going on holiday even though I always go on my own; I never know what to expect and I enjoy meeting people from around the country. Most of the time I find that I have something in common with them so I have lots to talk about, and it also gives me the chance to relax and not think about all the things that are stressing me out - I recharge myself and return home refreshed.

34. Nursing Home

When I got back, I visited mum straightaway; she was fine, and was really happy to see me back. I knew she was alright because I had rung every day to see how she was. When I saw mum's social worker, she gave me a booklet with a list of nursing homes which I could visit. I found this very hard, because mum was someone special in my life and I wanted the best home for her. I found two suitable local homes which I thought would meet mum's needs. One was round the corner from church so she could be pushed to church, and her cultural needs would have more chance of being met. My uncle, auntie, George and I went to visit these two homes and liked them both though mum of course wanted to be at home. In the end we all agreed to go for the one that would best be able to meet her needs. I wouldn't say I was really happy with the home she went into, and I never really felt comfortable with it; maybe at first I thought it was my feeling about mum going into a home that I hadn't dealt with yet.

I managed to go a whole year at work without having any time off, and was very proud of myself. I was still attending the hospital for the support group. I found it hard to concentrate on the discussions, though at times I didn't find it so difficult. I managed to form friendships with some of the girls in the group, and was put back on the waiting list for more therapy with a new therapist. I felt that it was going to take a while to form a relationship with her or to feel relaxed with her; this is important, yet I didn't want to form a close relationship with a therapist like I did the last time. I don't see how therapy can work if one cannot even form any sort of trust. All I could do was take one day at a time.

35. My Brother

I was still struggling with this illness even though I had had a good year at work, and I hadn't needed much support. I didn't want to become dependent on the people at the hospital, because I knew that what they had to offer me was not necessarily the answer. I was always encouraged to go back to church by my mum and other people and even more so by George who began to ask me to attend church with him. I still didn't feel ready to go yet, although a big part of me wanted to go with him. But George never gave up, and invited me to a big meeting in Birmingham with a well-known American preacher. I went with him and the meeting was alright. There were many people there which is what puts me off, because I think that everyone sees me as being fat, and I just hate it. George kept on inviting me to come to church with him, but I kept on making excuses, though I didn't want to be nasty to him because I knew he was trying to help me. Then one day George told me that he had been to a prayer meeting; and that he prayed for me at this meeting. He also gave me a cloth which had healing oil on it. It was at this stage that I realised how strong George's faith was. He also talked to me in a special way when he gave me that gift, suggesting that I should try to get myself better by reaching for goals in life and putting this illness behind me. If only it was as easy as that, I thought, but I took it on board anyway.

I thought about what George had said to me, and about the special healing cloth. I thought about what a strong man of God he had become, even though he had his own health problems. George had once been rushed to hospital when he collapsed at home because his blood pressure was very high. He spent a few weeks in hospital, and surgery seemed likely, but his condition became stable; he made a full recovery and went home. This illness had happened when mum was still well and at home, but it was very worrying for both of us.

Because George's faith was so strong, he made me think about my faith, and whether I wanted to revive it. I think for me it's about finding somewhere I could go and feel comfortable; I feel that faith is about a relationship with God not about the place you go, or about the people you go to church with. George also taught me that.

I was worried about mum's move to the nursing home; it took a while for her to settle in. I visited her every day; some days she seemed alright, other days she was really down. When I went to visit the home before mum went in there, they told me that they did activities with their residents, but when I asked mum what sort of things she did during the day, she said there was nothing going on. I was becoming more and more unhappy about her being there, but I wasn't sure what everyone else in the family thought. Mum had been there for about two months and she wasn't coping or settling down, and I didn't think that they were really looking after her. Instead of visiting, my therapist encouraged me to ring the home to check that mum was alright. I remained very worried about her, but I knew that there was nothing I could do.

It was a Sunday afternoon in early October. I had been to the gym for my workout, and I was just chilling out at home, listening to some music (the new Ce Ce Winans album). I was really enjoying listening to it, when I got a call from Sandra, who said that George had been rushed to hospital again. I asked what had happened, and she said that he had been to church, but when he came home he collapsed. I asked her to keep me informed, and I said I would be there as soon as I could. I did the usual things that I did on a Sunday. I visited mum. I didn't want to upset her or leave her very worried, so I played it down when I visited her and just said that George wasn't well. While I was with mum, Sandra rang me again to say that her mum had rung her from the hospital to say that George had had a brain haemorrhage and that he was very ill. They needed to move him to another hospital, because he needed to have an operation straightaway. I just said to mum that I would ring later, saying that I had to go because Sandra was crying on the phone and she had June and Tracey with her; I had to get to their house to support them as soon as possible. When I arrived at the house I brought them all to the hospital to be with their mum who was there on her own. She was in the waiting room, and said that they were getting George ready to be moved to the Q.E. Hospital where they would carry out the operation that George needed. We waited in the waiting room for about 15 minutes, and then a nurse came in to tell us that we could go in to see George before they moved him to Q.E.H. When we saw him he had been sedated and was just lying on the stretcher. Then we left to get to the other hospital as quickly as we could. When we arrived we were told which ward he would be on, so when we reached the ward George had already arrived and was being prepared for the theatre. We were then sent to the waiting room.

All we could do was to sit in the waiting room and wait for someone to come in to tell us what was happening. When I rang Mark he said that he was on his way. I also rang my uncle and let him know what was happening too. It seemed that we were waiting forever. Mark and another relative arrived and eventually a nurse came and told us that George was still in surgery; as soon as he was out, they would let us know. It was about 12 that night when the surgeon and a nurse came in and told us that George had had the operation; they had had to put a tube at the back of his head to stop the bleeding, and put him on a breathing machine. They said that as soon as he was ready, a nurse would call us, and we would be able to go in and see him. When they left, we were all speechless- we didn't know what to say to each other, for we knew that George was very ill.

Later we were able to see George in pairs and I went in with June. George was wired up to lots of machines that were keeping him alive. The nurse told us that we could go over and talk to George because he could still hear us. We didn't stay there long, and I soon drove the girls and their mum home.

I stayed awake all night, thinking about George, hoping and praying that everything would be alright. The morning couldn't come soon enough for me. When I rang the ward, the nurse said that he was comfortable, but even then I was still very worried about him. When I went to see mum, together with my aunt, I just had to reassure her the best way I could, but she was still really upset because she knew that her son was very ill.

The next few days were very hard. In my usual therapy session, I spent most of the session talking about George and what had happened to him. My therapist was worried about how it was affecting me; I just could not face food or drink, for I had too much going on in my head. I went to the support group, and I also had the odd phone call from church people. The next day I went to see George, but he was still very much sedated; they were hoping to slowly wake him up the same night. When I went to see him two days after the operation, he was awake; I said hello to him, and he put his hand up and waved to me to say hello. I asked him how he was feeling; he shook his head and touched the tube that was still in his throat.

He was still very sleepy, but he was sitting up, and he was able to respond to me when I spoke to him. It also was something positive for me to say to mum. When I visited her, I wondered whether to ask her about going to see George, but one of the carers advised me not to, because George was in intensive care and still very ill. She also thought that it would have been too upsetting for mum; I agreed and said I would take mum to the hospital when George was out of intensive care. The carer thought that would be a much better time.

Whenever I visited George over the first week, on some days he would respond better than others, but he had had major surgery so I knew that it would take time. In the second week of the illness, George took a turn for the worse, and when I visited him on 15th October 2003 he was unconscious. The nurse who was looking after him told me that he was not well and had not responded to anything. She also said that he might have had a stroke. When I left intensive care, I was in a daze. I attended the support group even though I wouldn't contribute much; I just needed to be there, so I could keep my mind off things. I was really worried about George and his condition, but the therapist who was leading the group emphasised how important it was to keep taking in fluid. I wasn't eating or drinking much nor was I getting much rest. After the group finished I went to visit mum. She seemed alright and asked me how George was; I said that he was not that well today, but I played it down as much as I could because I didn't want to worry mum too much. I didn't stay long with her, for I was too tired and I needed to get home to rest.

On the way home I had a call from Sandra, George's daughter, so I pulled off the road. She said that the doctors had told them that George was very ill and that he might not pull through. I just hung up and drove home. In the morning I was up and dressed by 6am but I waited until about 7am before ringing the hospital. The nurse told me that George was very ill, so I rang my cousin Kirsty and talked to her. I then rang Mark and spoke to him; he said that he would ring the hospital and see how George was; Kirsty said that she would ring me back too.

36. Losing Someone Special

It was about half-an-hour later that my brother rang me back. He asked if I was sitting down, and I said, "Yes, what's happened?" I could tell that something bad had happened, and then he said that George had died. I felt as if someone had thumped me in the chest. He said that he was going to the hospital to support my nieces and sister- in-law, and he would be with me soon. When I put the phone down I got up, then collapsed to the floor, banging my hands on the floor. I just lay there for a few minutes, then I got up and went upstairs and down again - I didn't know what I was doing at this stage. My cousins rang me and said that they were on their way. One of my cousins soon arrived. I was shocked, and very worried about how I would tell mum. My cousin said that Mark had rung her and said that he was coming here to see me and that we would all go together to tell mum.

We all went to the home together. Mark had already rung the home and talked to the nurse in charge, so when we got there they were expecting us. As soon as mum saw us, I could tell by the look on her face that she knew that we weren't bringing good news. When we told mum she was devastated. My niece Sandra rang me from the hospital and I said that we would be with her soon, so my cousin and Mark left to meet them at the hospital, but I didn't go with them because I wanted to stay with mum and I didn't want to see George's body. A lot of people came to see mum that morning. I stayed with mum all morning talking to her, saying that I couldn't understand why this had happened.

I had to leave mum in the afternoon but I told her that I would be back later, and then I went to see my sister- in-law and my nieces Sandra, June and Tracey. Going to George's house was really devastating, because the girls were really upset. June was upstairs in her room crying; all I could do was to hug her and say I was really sorry, though I knew that nothing that I said or did would make it alright for her. When I went back to see mum in the evening, she had more visitors with her, but my cousin Kirsty wanted me to stay with her, so I went back to her house that night.

That week was just so hard. George was only 46 years old and he was gone. The big brother who was always giving me advice about everything and was so strong. I could always rely on him for support, and whenever I phoned him and ask him about something, he would spend a long time replying. I always knew I could go to him, too. I don't know how his daughters would cope without their dad. They were only 6, 15 and 22 years old. I couldn't understand this, and became angry with God. Why did God do this? When my church friends spoke to me, all they said was that God knew best and that he had gone to a better place. I know that there is nothing that anyone can really say to comfort somebody, but to say that and just walk away is not really comforting nor is it helpful.

I spent the week doing things to prepare ourselves to say goodbye to George. Mum seemed to be coping with it all very well; when I told her how angry I was with God she said it was God's will, and I am sure that's how she got through the week. I wished that she had got the chance to see George in hospital, for she would have got a bit of comfort from seeing him, but it wasn't meant to be. I also went shopping for clothes and my auntie helped me to get some clothes for mum. I also helped my nieces. A lot of visitors came to their house; I had a lot of phone calls too. I didn't eat enough, being too busy running around. I was still very concerned about Mum and my nieces, wondering how they would cope with the funeral.

I slept at Kirsty's house on the night before the funeral. In the morning we both went to mum's Home, where Kirsty was going to do mum's hair and then take her in a taxi. I was going to drive to my sister- in-law's and join the funeral possession. When I arrived at the house, everyone seemed to be alright. The worst moment for me was when the cars arrived; that's when it really sunk in, and I just stood at the door looking. When we arrived at the church I went to the cars to see George's coffin. I don't know why I did that. I looked at all the flowers - mum's, mine and those from the kids. It just didn't seem real.

The funeral service was very nice. A lot of people were there - many friends whom he grew up with in the church, and from his new church. His daughter gave a lovely tribute, and his niece Jane sang a beautiful song. Mark and Sean read scriptures, and I gave a tribute to George too. At the end of the service we had the coffin opened so that everyone could view George if they wanted to. This was a horrible experience for everyone; I hadn't seen George at the hospital or at the Chapel of Rest so it was awful to see him in the coffin. It was hard for mum, his family and the rest of the family. Then the coffin was shut, and his body was carried out. At the cemetery I stood back while he was being buried, and because it was raining, it was decided that mum should go on to the hall where we all would be going for the meal after the funeral There were a lot of people there; it was lovely to see my uncle and his family from Huddersfield, because we didn't see them often. Many other people had come and they all got a chance to see mum too.

Afterwards I went back to the Home with mum. She was really poorly that night, and they had to phone for a doctor to see her, for she was vomiting and shaking. It must have been very hard for her to see her son and to be at his funeral - too much for her to cope with. The doctor gave her something for the sickness. The next day when I went to visit mum she was very quiet, and she didn't say much at all.

This stage is the hardest. People ring up and say what they have to say, but it is hard because all they say is that the person has gone to a better place, which makes me so angry- all I wanted was my big brother back. No one wants to hear about where they have gone, or that life goes on. We know all that. George was not expected to die, for he was only 46 years old. It was just so hard for all of us. I could see that his close friends found it hard to take in and understand too.

37. Trying To Cope Again

It was the 16th October 2003 when George died, and he was buried on the 31st October. It was the run-up to Christmas, which I dislike, finding it hard to cope with, but I tried really hard to get back into real life. When I did return to work, it was especially difficult because there were many parties, but I was determined to put the children first and put on a brave front. It wasn't easy, but I wanted to try and have some sort of normality in my life.

My sister- in-law and my nieces seemed to be coping; they didn't talk about loss. I think that we felt that it would be easier to carry on quietly, rather than to try to open up and say that we were missing him. I coped because I had to try to stay strong for mum, and I didn't want her to become ill again.

As soon as I returned to work, I also started again at the gym. My diet over the time of George's illness and death hadn't been good; I just fitted in a snack with a drink at the end of the day. There was so much going on, and I had so many things to sort out. I was trying to look after mum and George's family, so I just couldn't stop or even think about food. This concerned my therapist, who wanted me to try day care; she suggested this while we were planning George's funeral, but I thought this was a bad idea because there was far too much to do on the day of the funeral. My sessions with the therapist didn't continue after George's death, because I was new to that therapist and we hadn't done much work together.

The first Christmas after George died was hard because I spent it with his family and also spent a lot of time with mum. I visited the graves, dad's and George's, which were in the same cemetery. I went to dad's grave first, then to George's - the first time that I had visited his grave since he had been buried. It was difficult and very upsetting but I needed to be there so that I could think about George and the good times that we had shared. I think Christmas always makes me think about dad and I miss him more, and think about him more at this time of year; this year I was thinking about both of them and missing them a lot; but I knew that I still had mum and that it was harder for her because she couldn't be around to support George's family like I could. This makes up a big part of Christmas, with the focus on the family.

After the Christmas break, going back to work was easy because I just wanted to try to carry on the best way I could. My friends at work encouraged me a lot; Rosie also was always at the end of the phone, and Catherine was there too if I needed her. Catherine had not long lost her dad, and she talked to me about how she felt. She had been very close to him, and many times she would be in tears, which I found very uncomfortable and hard.

I found it difficult when Catherine was talking to me because it wasn't something that I was used to. In my culture one doesn't talk about death, or mental health and that's why I got frustrated and angry. The answer to someone's death is always that they have gone to a better place. I became so angry, confused, and frustrated that I forgot how to smile, or show my feelings, since it was taken to be a sign of weakness. I know it's hard to talk about loss, but I feel it is an important part of grieving because if you don't talk about the loss how can you just get on with life? It will haunt you forever.

I didn't know what to do with all these feelings. I could only keep my anger down by eating as little as possible and exercising excessively. This blocked everything out, and I found that I could cope with everything a lot better. But dad and George had now gone, and I was supposed to feel alright about it all, and stop feeling sorry for myself. I was so angry that I could have punched someone.

AM I TAKING CONTROL OR IS THE EXERCISE CONTROLLING ME?

38. Running

I found that when I was training all these feelings disappeared; it was nice to be exercising in the fresh air and I now really enjoyed running. I also met a lot of people through joining a running group, and it was really nice running and chatting. I ran about 6 races and found I was becoming very competitive, especially when I ran in races for a charity or an organisation. I began to go to the gym, as well as running twice a week. When I was running I saw myself in a different light, believing that I was capable of being just as good as anyone else when I used my inner strength. I also discovered that George had been an excellent runner. He used to run in a Birmingham running club, and there were a lot of trophies around the house which he had won. So I also wanted to do well for him.

I used running to control my weight and my body shape, but with all the exercise that I was doing I was beginning to have medical problems. I was in the gym exercising one morning before work when I suddenly started to have pains in my chest. After 10 minutes I stopped my exercise programme because I was feeling sick. I stopped and I left the gym, aware that something was wrong. This wasn't the first time that I had felt like this; my chest would feel really tight, and I wasn't sure what was happening.

I had once entered a 10k race which I wasn't really looking forward to, running with two friends. I knew that I was more than capable of running this distance, so I knew that I wasn't pushing myself too hard. I started the race and was running very comfortably for the first half-an-hour, and then all of a sudden, I began to feel really sick. I continued running, only to collapse, ending up on the floor with someone asking me if I was alright. I just felt so stupid and embarrassed; I was so disappointed with myself for not being able to complete the race. I was taken to the first aid room where they checked my pulse; the problem occurred because it was a really warm day and I had a thick t-shirt on. They also said that I was really fit, because of my pulse reading, but I knew that something was wrong; in addition I was having a lot of trouble with my periods, which were irregular and really heavy. I also had hot flushes on and off.

I finally decided to book a doctor's appointment, and I

explained to her how I felt and what was happening. She sent me off for a blood test, but it took a week before the results came. While I was waiting for the results, I still went to the gym to exercise, and I also still kept running, for I was really enjoying the running group and I didn't want to stop. After a week, I rang the doctor's to check on the results, and was told that I was very anaemic and I needed to come and see the doctor. I did so, and she put me on iron tablets, telling me to go back a few weeks later for another test. I asked her about the other test concerning my periods. She said that the test showed that I only had a few eggs. When I asked her if I would be able to have children, she said that she would refer me to a specialist who would be able to do more tests and answer my questions.

The only person I really spoke to about how I was starting to feel physically was my mum, who was able to listen and give me advice. She was more settled now, although she was never fully happy at the Home. I was concerned about their care regarding clothes for mum; they all had name tags sewn on, but whenever I went to visit her she was in different clothes, or someone else's. Also she was always left downstairs on her own until god knows what time, when she was put to bed. The whole set-up of the place really upset me. I still visited mum every day, and felt very worried about her. She had been there for a year from summer 2003, and it was now summer 2004 and there had been the death of George in October 2003. Maybe it was too soon for a move. In my culture it is seen as a weakness to seek advice from others, and you have to suffer in silence. But I really felt a failure in my community. Why can't I eat? Why do I have to go to the gym? It just made me so ANGRY.

39. My Health Problems

I decided to wait for a few months to see how mum settled and how she seemed in herself. I was still having problems with my exercising, and wasn't feeling well. I was taking the iron tablets which didn't seem to be making much difference, so the doctor sent me to have another blood test. When the results of that test came back, it showed that my blood count was a lot lower than the first test, so the doctor increased the amount of iron tablets that I needed to take each day. This was again monitored, and I had to go back in a few weeks. I also talked to the doctor about my chest pains; the doctor referred me to a heart specialist so I could have tests done. The appointment for me to see the doctor about my menopause symptoms also came through. I attended the appointment, and was weighed by the nurse, which I hated; I always tell them not to show me or tell me how much I weighed, but she always did so. I went to see the doctor who had sent me for my blood test, and he said that he would see me again in one or two months, when we had received the results of my test. I was becoming really tired, and was always feeling sleepy. As soon as I came in from work, I would sit down and fall asleep, and if I wasn't at work I would sleep for most of the day. The next blood test showed my blood count had gone down again, so I was referred to another specialist. I was now seeing a total of four specialists: one for my eating disorder, one for my women's problems, one for my anaemic problem, and one for my heart.

It was really hard to keep up with my appointments. The next appointment was for me to see the heart specialist, who did more tests- an E.C.G (which was fine), and an x-ray of my heart, which showed that it was large due to the fact that I did a lot of exercise. I had a 24 hour "tape and scan" check of my heart, which was fine, and when the specialist knew just how anaemic I was, he thought that was what caused the chest pains. The results of my women's check showed that I was going through the menopause. When the doctor told me, I was really upset. I asked him if this had anything to do with the eating disorder, but he said that it didn't. He asked me when I started to have my period, and I said I was 9 years old. He said if I started my periods when I was 15 I would have gone into my menopause at a later age, but because I started when I was so young my body had just changed naturally - the eating disorder wouldn't have made any difference. This made me feel a bit better. The specialist I saw about my anaemia gave me various tests, which were all clear, but to get my blood count back to normal I had to have three rounds of iron infusions.

I was so relieved when all the results came back, because I had never seen myself as being ill, only having an eating disorder. Because I am not underweight, my body mass index was alright, and that is what matters; that's how you are put into a box. The other thing which really worried me and got my back up, was when everyone said I looked so well. This means to me that they are saying that I look fat and ugly, and I hate that statement. What do they mean? I guess it means that there can't possibly be anything wrong with me, because of the way they see me.

40. Trying To Take Control Of My Life

I was again sent a letter to see another therapist; I felt that I could connect with her and I liked the way she worked with me because she set me tasks to do. I was getting really down because I had a lot of feelings that I had to clear up with my dad's death and now George's. I visited dad's and George's graves and I wrote down my feelings in a diary, on the 5th May 2005; *"I'm with dad in a way, - I'm at the grave trying to remember the happy times, but still feeling numb with pain and a great sense of loss. I just wish I had done more for dad when he was around. I wish I had told him how much he meant to me. Maybe if I had done so this time wouldn't have been so hard and painful for me; maybe if I hadn't started this stupid diet, I would have been able to feel something and I would have been able to grieve for him"*

"At George's grave, I feel so sad - there is just so much grief, it just feels horrible being here, I wish I was dreaming and I was not really here. I never understood why you were taken away at only 46. I miss the way you always thought you could work everything out and were always there for me. Even if I never listened to you that never stopped you. I remember your smile and your laugh".

I had lost two special people who had a great part in my life; two people whom I loved and cared for so much. This double loss affects me every day. I felt that my friendships suffered a lot because of my mood swings, which could be caused by my eating disorder; I often wanted to eat normally. I wished that I could just go to bed, wake up in the morning and have a full English breakfast and everything would be back to how it was before I started this diet. But that never happened, and it was never going to work like that. Yes, I got a lot of support from my therapists but I don't really think that therapy helped me; I find it very hard to open up. I really struggled in my therapy sessions because I didn't know how to express my feelings. I made sure that I attended all my sessions; it was hard, because I always got the question about making changes. Yes, I wanted to change, but I was hurting inside and I couldn't express it. Whenever I tried to eat or to stop exercising, it hurt even more, and the feelings and the thoughts were harder to deal with. My friends thought, "She doesn't want to get better, she doesn't want to help herself. She's a waste of time." But I desperately wanted to get well again, but every time I tried to break the cycle of not eating during the day, or if I had a drink, I felt that I was a bad person and I didn't deserve it. Therapy is the way to help but I still feel bad and weak about going to see a therapist, because it's not the normal thing to do in my community. I was often asked questions like, "What are you going there for? Do you need to attend hospital? How can we help you?" Some of the questions had a point because yes I have got to do this for myself, and I am fully aware of that, but some of the questions were just stupid because if I didn't need to go to hospital I wouldn't be wasting my time and theirs. If I could sort this out by just eating I would do that.

My job suffered because I had a lot of time off due to the illness, which did not help me and my fellow workers. I loved my job, working with children, and watching them develop from one stage to the next, which I really enjoyed. I loved working with the parents. It felt great when I was on the floor working with the children, talking to them, developing their language and just interacting with them. The job is very rewarding. The responsibility is great; I understand that, and it's not a job you can do if you aren't 100%. I have always tried to do my best and know I have fallen short because of illness. This has put pressure on the others, which I greatly regret.

I was really struggling and having a lot of time off work because of my health. I was not sleeping very well at night; instead, I was sleeping for most of the day maybe because my body didn't know what was going on. I think that my consultant was getting concerned about my health, so it was suggested that I should give day care a go, which I did. It was the same format as before. It was hard, but it was worth giving it another go. The most important thing that I gained from going into day care was that I realised that I needed to go to Cruse for some bereavement counselling, and this was like a breakthrough for me. When I rang Cruse they were very nice; they told me that I would have an appointment to be assessed first, and then I would be given a counsellor who would work through things with me. I was pleased that I had contacted them, and was ready to begin. I stayed in day care for 3 weeks, which may not have helped my eating disorder, but at least for once I had begun to tune into my emotional problems.

A month later I spoke to the counsellor who was assessing me. She was very nice and made me feel relaxed and comfortable. She said that it would take a few months before I heard from them, but they would get back in touch with me as soon as possible. I was seeing the therapist from the hospital and that was going well; she was getting me to work out things that I wanted to change in the short-term and the things I wanted to change long-term, and we would tick each goal off as we went along. The long-term goals seemed hard to achieve, though the short-term goals were more achievable. We also looked at and talked about death a little, and about mum, and about how I was coping at work.

My goals were to become a foster career, and to be able to have a drink without the feeling of guilt. I wanted a better body image, and to feel positive about myself. I needed confidence, and wanted to simply have a snack during the day. I needed to feel acceptance within myself, and of course I would always be a fitness fanatic, wanting to complete a half marathon! I decided that I needed more of a challenge in my career- a new occupation maybe- and the one thing that everyone says they want to do: enjoy life to the full!

I wished that I could talk to mum about how I felt but I knew that she was struggling. All she wanted to do was to return home. I was not happy for her to be in the Home either. Mum started showing signs of being ill again, becoming very confused – she would talk about people that I didn't know; maybe she knew them when she was growing up in Jamaica. On the odd occasion she would become loud, singing loudly. It frustrated me when no one picked up on things like that. Time and time again I would have to go to the care staff and point this out. Mum was with them all day and they didn't know how confused she was, even though they had her medical records. At last mum was assessed by someone from the Q.E.P.H, and they said that she needed to go into hospital. She was taken into the Q.E.P.H and put in the ward she was in last time, which was good for her because she knew most of the staff and they knew her.

It always made me very sad when mum became so unwell and had to go into hospital. I think that she was suffering from a lot of grief herself, because she didn't like to talk about her losses, and when I tried to tell her how I felt, she became very uncomfortable. I knew her faith was strong, and maybe that's how she wanted to leave it; so I never pushed it, not wanting to upset her.

41. My Exercise Diary

I continued to go to the gym every day as a way of controlling my weight. I was still eating late in the evening because my days were so busy, with work all day, then the gym, then visiting mum in the evening. By the time I had done all that it was about 8:30-9:00pm, so I just ate any rubbish just to keep me going until the next day. I just hated food, so I wasn't going to waste time in the kitchen cooking a big meal. I also found it hard to shop for food; I tended to get one thing for a meal i.e. a chicken breast or salad on its own. To me this was a meal, plus something to drink with it, and also some rice tea biscuits for a snack. If I ate more than that I would make myself work harder at the gym to make up for it, and I hated myself even more for eating so much.

I had to stop running because of all the problems I was having with my health. I really missed running and the running club when I had got to know many people. I started to do some spinning classes, and also do circuits which are good for all-round fitness. I also took tennis lessons with Rosie every week - great fun and energetic too. My therapist got me to record just how much exercise I took, the sort of exercise it was, and how long I spent on each piece of equipment. I found this very helpful because it made me see just how much exercise I was doing as recorded in the chart:

My Exercise Diary: Autumn 2004

Day	Time	Venue	Activity	Duration
Monday	7am	Gym	Cross Trainer	1 hour 15mins
	4:30pm	Gym	Cross ramp/ Trainer Running machine Rower Machine, Weights and sit-ups	45mins 25mins 18mins
Tuesday	7am	Gym	Cross Trainer	1 hour 15mins
	5:10pm	Gym	Cross Ramp, Treadmill Rower Machine, Weights, sit-ups	50mins 20mins 10mins
Wednesday	7am	Gym	Cross Trainer	1 hour 15mins
	6pm	Gym	Cross Ramp/ Trainer Treadmill	1 hour 25mins
Thursday	7am	Gym	Cross Trainer	1 hour 15mins
	5:30pm	Gym	Cross ramp/ Trainer Treadmill, Rower Spinning Class	40mins 25mins 10mins 1 hour class
Friday	7am	Gym	Cross Trainer	1 hour 10mins
	5pm	Gym	Treadmill Rowing machine Cross Ramps, Weights and sit ups	20mins 14mins 50mins
Saturday	8am	Gym	Cross Trainer Cross Ramp/ Trainer Treadmill, Weights, Sit-ups Spinning Class	1 hour 10mins 40mins . 20mins 1 hour class
Sunday	9:50am	Gym	Cross Trainer	1 hour

This was my weekly exercise routine. Most of the time I really enjoyed it, though sometimes it could be very hard because I got very tired, but I kept to it because I knew that I would be burning calories and I didn't want to end up as big as I was before.

My therapist suggested to me that I should do five minutes less each day in the gym, which I tried. But soon I would say to myself, "I might as well do another 10 minutes", so that idea never worked with me. The only other way that it might work was to stick to the classes which only lasted for an hour. I am addicted to exercising; and if I don't go to the gym I feel very guilty; I feel that I have to make up for it the next day by doing more in the gym- but this is something that I will have to change.

My work with this therapist was very positive, for she made me look at things on paper, which I found a lot better, even though it was really difficult because I was hurting, angry and very, very bitter. I found working with the therapist good, but I knew she could only work with me for a maximum of 2 years.

While I was seeing my therapist I began to have second thoughts about seeing someone from Cruse. When I told them they just said that I could get in touch with them when I felt that I was ready to do so.

42. Mum's New Home

When mum became ill again and had to go back into hospital, it took a while before she began to get better. Sometimes she seemed a bit upset, but that settled down very quickly, and I was very happy with the staff on the ward because most of them knew her very well and I could see that mum responded very well to them. I hated seeing mum ill with such a really unpleasant illness.

I could see that mum's treatment was going very well, and I began to think about her future treatment. I spoke to her social worker about moving her, but he wasn't happy about it, even when I told him about my concerns about the Home she was in. I started to look around for a new nursing home, but when I told them about mum's medical conditions some of them didn't want to know, which I thought was wrong. I spoke to her social worker about this and he said that not all Homes accept residents who have additional medical needs. This was a bit disappointing and hard to hear. I wanted the best for my mum so I carried on looking by phoning different Homes. I knew I had to start looking at nursing homes out of the Birmingham area, because I knew I would still be able to visit mum by car.

All this was taking up a lot of time. Mum had made really good progress, and as far as the staff were concerned she was ready to be discharged, and the consultant also wanted to arrange a discharge date for her. I explained that I was looking for a new Home for her, but he wasn't interested, saying that mum should go back to the present nursing home. I wasn't really happy with that, knowing that she didn't want to go there again.

I just had to carry on looking for a new Home. Even if she had to go back to that Home she wasn't going to stay there for very long and this was all really getting me down. I was so busy working, going to the gym, and visiting different nursing homes. Moreover, I didn't feel that the professional agency involved with mum understood how important it was for her to be moved. I would have thought that if mum wasn't happy, or at least comfortable, at a Home, then it would have a knock-on effect on her mental health. I knew that mum wanted to be at home, but that was never going to be possible. Soon things changed, however, for I had a phone call from mum's nursing home; and the manager and one of the nurses went to visit mum in hospital. I knew mum's physical needs were many; she needed a hoist to get her in and out of bed, and also for her personal needs. I knew that she had become weaker since she had gone into hospital, but I didn't think that things had changed that much. I think everything worked out well in the end, because nobody wanted her to go back to that Home, and I now had a bit more time to look around.

I managed to find two nursing homes which would accept mum, one of which was in Great Barr, which was about half-an-hour away from the house, though it would take longer at peak times. The nurse in charge was really nice, the rooms were big, and the Home would be able to meet mum's needs. The only problem was that they didn't have any vacancies. The nurse in charge said that I could visit the Home again and she would let me know if a room came up. There was also the other Home in the Sandwell area, which a bit nearer to the house. They did have a room available and mum could move in any time, but I preferred the first home. I visited both Homes again with Kirsty, and she also liked the first Home. Mum's social worker contacted the home in Smethwick, and the nurse in charge came to visit mum in the hospital. She was happy to accept mum; and I was very happy to hear that. But I was disappointed that the other home had no places.

This amazing Home had two floors; on both floors there was a large sitting-room with a television. The floors also had a dining area connected to the lounge, and the bedrooms were all on the same floor as the lounge. The rooms were quite big with a large wardrobe, an en-suite, and a dressing-table. There were bathrooms and showers on the same floor, which was really nice. I really liked the nursing home, and felt happier than I did with the other Home. I now felt less anxious about mum moving into this Home, and I started to feel a bit more relaxed.

The only thing that worried me about mum moving into the Home was the fact that she had not been there to see it herself. This was only because the doctors had said that it wouldn't be possible for her to do that. I just had to hope that she liked it. A discharge date had been given for mum to move to the new nursing home – 24th December 2004. I would have preferred it to be after Christmas; but that was, maybe more about me. Anyway, mum moved to her new nursing home, and when I visited she looked happy and comfortable. I brought all her clothes and some pictures and some things from home- her sheets, vases, television, tape recorder and CD player, as much as I could to make her feel as comfortable as possible. I thought that she was going to have a difficult Christmas, but she seemed to be really happy. When I asked her how she felt about the nursing home, she said that she liked the home and that the staff were really nice. I was really happy about that; and so far everything seemed to be going well; mum had a good Christmas, with quite a few visitors. My brother Mark visited and he seemed quite happy about the nursing home.

I still worried about mum but not as much as before. I felt that I could now concentrate more on myself and my job. I was now beginning to realise the real cause of my problems – whenever I ate something I felt dirty inside; I saw food as being my enemy. Every time I looked in the mirror, I saw a fat, ugly person who didn't deserve anything. I got up every morning and the same thought went through my head "I shouldn't eat today; eat as little as I can today; I am fat." I would be in the gym or at an exercise class and I would see everyone around me (ladies) and I would think that they were thin, "Why can't I be thin like them; they have good figures; don't eat, you aren't allowed to eat anything." These thoughts would drive me mad, and I wanted to go away for a break; I felt that I was losing it. I found that eating with people was so difficult because I felt that they were just watching me, looking at the amount of food I was eating and thinking that I was greedy and fat.

I just couldn't see a way out of this awful illness. I just felt that I was trapped- caught in a dark tunnel. I was trying to dig my way out of the tunnel, but the more that I dug the more I was getting stuck. My friends said that all I had to do was just eat. I don't think people realised that to solve or to recover from an eating disorder doesn't happen if you just simply eat; it is so much more than that. I struggled with my eating every day because I was not sorting my inner feelings out. I also felt that I had to take control of something; for my life was a mess, with everything that had gone on in the last few years.

43. Goals for 2005

I hoped that 2005 would be a different year; a year when I could make positive changes; especially now that mum had settled well in the new nursing home. I would try harder to get myself better, though I was not attending the support group anymore because they now met on a different night. At least I was still seeing my therapist who helped me to write my goals down on paper. I wrote in my diary on the 20th January 2005. *"I'm feeling really low at the moment finding these things very hard:*

1. *I feel really tired, and on my last legs. It's not because I am doing too much. I am still visiting mum at the weekend and a few times during the working week. I suppose I am not sleeping very well.*
2. *I feel really bad about the way I look. I hate my body; it makes me feel sick and angry. I just want to close the rest of the world down; they don't understand me, and they are just making me feel angry.*
3. *Why have they invited me for a meal – when am I going to eat a three-course meal?*
4. *Dad's anniversary is not far away. I have been thinking a lot about him over the past few weeks. I had a dream about him and George; it was a very strange dream. With time the pain is getting better, but I have never got over losing them, and I still miss them so much every day.*

I also wrote my goals down:

Short Term Goals

- Snacking during the day (maintain a diet with iron).
- Phone call to fostering agency.
- Drinking during the day.
- Snacking with friends.
- Book SPICE (social, activity, sports and adventure group) events.

- Lose weight.

Medium Term Goals

- Start looking at jobs.
- Work with Cruse.
- Re-new my faith.

- Let friends and family help.

Long Term Goals

- Make fostering application.
- Start reducing exercise.
- More self-confidence.

- Like/accept myself.

- Be positive about my body.

- Change jobs.
- Run half marathon.
- Enjoy life to the full.

Some of them I knew would be long-term goals, some of them short-term, but I knew I could achieve them. These were goals that I set for myself, not suggested by my therapist. When I started to look at my goals I felt that eating and drinking during the day would be a real struggle, because I felt that it wouldn't work.

I felt really down; I really wanted to change but I just

didn't know what to do next. I wasn't going to give up on treatment though; I knew that I would have a lot of work to do. I wrote in my diary on the 7ᵗʰ March 2005: *"I feel that the one sad thing about all of this is that I am still trying to find a way out. I feel that this illness has become my friend, my comforter, and my way of coping with stress."*

I realised that my eating disorder was now my best friend, and it has never really let me down. I have had a lot of people in my life over the last few difficult years who have come along and said silly things, like, "All you have to do is just eat," as if it was that easy. But I could rely on my eating disorder through the good times and the bad, because it never let me down.

I sometimes feel that the best way forward with this illness is just to carry on and pretend that I have no problem. I haven't got an eating disorder because I don't look as if I have a problem. I look fat, whereas to have an eating disorder you have to be 5 stone with body mass index of 10. The way some people have spoken makes me sick and angry. All I can do is to take one day at a time and just do the best I can.

MOVING
FORWARD

44. Mum's 79th Birthday

The good thing was that mum was a lot happier now, and I arranged a birthday party for her 79th birthday; it was just a small party with her close family friends, held at the nursing home. It was so funny at the time because mum was fast asleep when everyone arrived, so we were all sitting around waiting for her to wake up. I was beginning to think that she was never going to wake up, but she did eventually open her eyes and look around at everyone. She had the most beautiful smile and said what a nice party. A few weeks later I took her to church; this was good for mum because she hadn't been to church since she had become ill. She was a very strong Christian, and her faith through all her illness never weakened.

I often wondered, "If I had God in my life, would I have this illness? Would I feel the way I feel inside?" Maybe if I was a strong Christian I would not have the problems that I have today. On the other hand I thought that maybe there was a reason why all this was happening, a sort of punishment? I didn't know if going back to church would help, but I was just not ready yet.

45. My Thoughts

There was a special person who made me laugh; I could talk to him about anything, and we liked similar things. But I knew all we could be was just friends. He took me to the theatre to watch 'Tommy' which I really enjoyed. I loved the theatre, but I felt bad about going, and I also felt guilty about going with him. It was just too complicated and I didn't need any more stress in my life. This made me sad because he was such a nice guy. This helped me see how my thoughts could be positive as well as negative; I could also see how this affected my eating disorder.

I continued to have my battle with this illness. At work things were going all right until my eating disorder on a bad day affected my work colleagues, because of my mood swings (due to the lack of food, or so they said). But in general things were going well. The co-coordinator of the unit I worked in was leaving to go and live in Australia. I had a really good relationship with her and I was going to miss her a lot. A temporary co-coordinator for the unit was needed. I thought about it and decided to apply for the job; I had nothing to lose. It would be good for my confidence and career, and if I got the job it would boost my possibilities for future jobs. I had an interview and thought I did really well; though I did really well, I didn't think I had done well enough to get the job. But the fact that I tried was a boost for me. I wasn't appointed, but I wasn't upset about it all, as another role was offered to me. I was really pleased about that and excited, because it was a positive step. This was offered in the summer and I worked in that role for about two months, but then I was transferred into another role. I was really hurt by this and wrote in my diary August 2005:

"Being given a new role gave me confidence; I was pleased and quite proud of myself having confidence in my ability to do this job, and although in the last 12 months there have been a lot of changes at work (a new building, new staff, and the co-coordinator leaving,) it has brought out the best in me." I had been left to run the unit at times which I quite enjoyed; it had helped me develop new abilities and gain in confidence. I still struggled with my eating disorder, but I had been able to put this aside and put my job in front. I think it's because I was feeling so good about myself. I had feared that it might go wrong - that I

would not be able to contribute to the team at the team meetings and that that would affect me. But now everything was taken away without anyone telling me or even talking to me about it. I was so stressed and worried, after previously feeling that I was high on a mountain because I was very confident – but then someone came along and just pushed me off. The only way forward in all of this was to try and think positively and to write down my fears and worries.

What Are My Worries And Fears

1) Being watched in the new unit.
2) Not being able to work as well as I know I can.
3) Being challenged wrongly.
4) Feeling and fearing that I wasn't going to be successful with report writing, planning, parents' interviews, etc
5) Fitting into a new team, will I be able to feel a part of that team?

46. The Way Forward

"I must do the job as best as I can and just try to be positive. I am going to try my best to do my job and not to fail." I was very worried that I wouldn't be able to fit into the team. I just had to try, because at the end of the day I had to choose. The first few weeks were hard but I did my best. I wrote in my diary on 11th September 2005: *"I felt I had to take some laxatives today, I feel so down."* I couldn't cope with this anymore. I felt better after taking 10 laxatives, however.

I was going back into the illness again, feeling that I needed to punish myself to numb the way that I was feeling. The one good thing that I did was to book a holiday in Gran Canaria, so at least I had that to look forward to. I knew that when I got like this I ate less, and the exercising was more punishing. I had so much anger inside me that I couldn't get it out and it was difficult to find people I trusted and could talk to. All I could do was go to work every day, do the job the very best I could, and try my best to fit into the new unit, communicating with the staff, children and parents. My emotions were all over the place. October was coming up, and 16th October would be the first anniversary of George's death, but at least I would be away on holiday. I had mum's equipment set up in the front room in the hope that she was going to come home. They hadn't collected the equipment when she went into the nursing home and it was still there. The hospital didn't want the equipment back, which was a real waste. It had taken me 3 years to decide to sort out the equipment and the room, and although it was hard, I knew that I had to do it. The staff workers at the nursing home were going to talk to the manager and would arrange for someone to take the equipment away; so I wouldn't have to worry about that.

I felt that that was a positive step for me, but I was still so stressed and down about everything; I wasn't sleeping very much, and I was having strange dreams about dad and George. I had a dream about me being killed with a gun. I couldn't understand where these weird dreams were coming from - they really scared me. I knew that George's anniversary was in a few days time, and that might be why I was having all these dreams. I felt really angry and upset, but I wasn't sure why I was so angry and upset.

47. 2005 Events

I set off on my holiday, hoping to recharge my batteries, because I was really tired; I hadn't been getting any sleep, being so stressed. But I knew that mum was happier now she was in a good place, where the staff were nice. Even so, I rang the Home every night, or during the day, to make sure.

I had not been to the Canary Islands so I was very excited; the apartment was nice and comfortable, and the scenery was lovely. It was a bit noisy at night, but I got used to it in the end. Every night at about 1am the music would eventually stop, so I was able to get some sleep. I made a lot of day trips, one being a survival day trip. I also visited different parts of the island to do some more sightseeing. On a boat trip to spot dolphins we were lucky and saw loads of dolphins. It was great seeing them swimming in the water, because they looked so free and beautiful. I did a lot of shopping and walking, maybe to make sure I used up a lot of calories. I made sure I didn't eat much food and I would just buy some items like sandwiches and bottled drinks. I met a lot of very nice people and it was very hot even though it was October. I phoned the nursing home every day to make sure mum was alright - she was fine, and I was looking forward to seeing her again. I also went to a local bar to watch the football; England were playing a qualifying match, and there was a really good atmosphere there. I had a fantastic holiday. While I was away I made a few decisions about things that I felt I had to change. I decided that when I was at work I would just go and do my job and try not to get involved with what everyone else was doing. I also decided to join an activity club where I could do group activities with people.

I also wondered whether a new environment would be better, because I just felt physically, mentally and emotionally drained. I had so much hurt inside me and I just couldn't get it out.

The first thing I did when I got back was to visit mum; she was fine, and really happy to see me. There had been no problems whilst I had been away. I told her what I had done, and how enjoyable it had been. It was hard when I went back to work, however, for I was still trying to settle into the team. I suppose I had only just joined the team and I had to give it time. I was still working with my therapist; she was still getting me to work on my feelings and how I felt about myself and why I felt that I didn't deserve anything. I found this type of work was very hard. One thing that I realised while I was away was that I still had a lot of work to do about my feelings. I have found that I had so many strong feelings, like guilt, and the feeling that I deserved nothing and I needed to be punished. I feel that is why I am so stuck in this illness. I used to think that if I went to day care I would be sorted out; or when I was an in-patient that would make me better, but this was going to take a while to untangle. It was not something that would just go away. I was getting very impatient and frustrated, and I hated feeling the way I did.

I had a good therapist, but I knew that she couldn't do it for me. But I just had to keep trying for my mum's sake. She deserved to have as good a Christmas as I could make for her. I made plans for mum to go to church near Christmas. I organised a taxi to pick us both up and take us to church. I also arranged to take mum to the local shopping complex, which I thought would be nice for her.

The nurse came to see me when I was visiting mum, and said that they would collect the equipment which was in the house. I was very pleased, and arranged for the room to be cleared out and decorated after Christmas. I was pleased that I had managed to sort it out, and that the equipment could now be used; it seemed a real waste of brand new equipment otherwise.

Christmas week was going to be very busy. Mum's party was on the Thursday before Christmas; I was able to attend the party, which I really enjoyed, and mum had a good time too. After the party I had to do a lot of shopping, because I wanted to do the usual shopping for mum's nieces, nephews and grandchildren. I also had to get cards for mum's close friends in church. It was a pleasure to be doing all of this for mum on the Saturday, even though I didn't feel very well.

I had to get up very early, for I had lots to do. A group from a local church was coming to visit mum to encourage her. It was like a prayer meeting. I arranged this with the nursing home and they were happy for this to happen. The group sang some songs and they prayed and read some scripture verses to her. She enjoyed this very much. After that, Sean, Jane and I went shopping with mum and I bought some things for her that she could take back to the Home with her. Finally, a taxi collected us and brought us back to the Home.

On Sunday I took mum to church in the morning, and she enjoyed the service, as usual. We got to church at 11.00 a.m. and everyone was happy to see Mum. They all came over to say hello together with big hugs and kisses. We got back to the nursing home at 1.30 p.m, just in time for her dinner. I had Tracey and Paul with me, as I was taking them to the cinema in the afternoon, and we were going to have dinner afterwards, so I didn't stop with mum for long. I just saw her settled, and then I left.

The kids enjoyed both the cinema and the meal afterwards, before I took them home. The next day was Monday, and I took Sean and Jane to Warwick Park for ice-skating. This was great fun, even though none of us could ice skate, and we all had a brilliant time. I was now looking forward to Christmas Day, though it always brought back memories and I always felt like I had to lie through the whole day, or make excuses, just to get through the whole Christmas period.

On Christmas Day I woke up at 7.00 a.m. and watched a bit of television whilst I wrapped up all my presents, and then packed them into my car. I left the house at 9.30 a.m. I wanted to visit dad and George's graves. I always feel I have to visit their graves at this time of year because I think about them so much. Although I feel down afterwards, in another sort of way I feel better for going. I popped round to my friend's house afterwards to drop off her card and present, but I only stayed for a very short time.

I then came back home to change my clothes and freshen up a bit, because I was going to see my mum. I got there at 1.00 pm and it was really nice, because they had the music going in the background as they were getting ready for the Christmas dinner. One of the carers gave me a cracker to pull with mum, and we pulled it together. I put mum's hat on her, and I had to wear mine. Mum was really happy - we both were. I helped mum with her dinner, but when the staff offered me dinner I said no. I gave mum her presents and left at 4.00 pm, telling my mum that I was going to see Mark, but that I would try to get back later. I got to Mark's around 4.30 pm, and it was great to be there because Sean, Jane and Paul were very excited because of all the presents they received. I had a drink while I was there. All the family were going to visit mum so I said I would go back with them. Mum enjoyed having her children and grandchildren around her, and we all stayed until 6pm, when I left to visit Kelly and my nieces; I had a nice evening with them too. I got home around 9.30 p.m, really tired, for I had had a really busy day.

The one thing that I miss about Christmas is when the family gets together and has a special meal, although I couldn't allow myself to eat now. On Boxing Day my mum would make a feast. She would cook a 12lb Turkey, with white rice, macaroni cheese (it was my job to make it.), beef, sweetcorn, peas, roast potatoes, sprouts, salad and gravy. For dessert we had ice cream, fruit salad and jelly.

About one hour later mum would offer everyone cake and biscuits, even though by this time everyone was bursting. Those were the days when I used to enjoy Christmas; nowadays they are so different. I always worry about the amount of food that is around, fearing that I will overeat and put on a lot of weight. Now on Christmas Day I just have a drink, but I may have a few treats when I visit friends or family just to be in the Christmas spirit.

48. My Promise
To Myself: 2006

I didn't do anything to see the New Year in, but I made some decisions like we all do at the beginning of each year. I think that the New Year is a time to reflect on the old year and look to the future. I wrote in my diary 2nd January 2006: *"I am going to make a lot of changes this year. I am going to stop eating all these packed dinners (they are just making me gain weight and bloat me up). I need to lose weight and tone up. I am also going to change jobs, because I feel I have a lot to offer."*

I always hoped that my eating disorder would just disappear, but it was with me every day. It was my best friend, which I could depend on; it was telling me all the time that I was fat and I needed to lose weight. When I was in the gym, I would look at other people and I would think that they had great toned bodies. Why can't I be like them, for everybody around me had wonderful bodies except me. I was the only one who needed to lose weight. At times these thoughts just drove me mad. I hated them and would get really angry with myself, and end up telling myself to stop it. I hated food, and after going all day with no food, I would have the same thoughts that I was greedy or fat and needed to go to the gym to exercise and get rid of the food because I was so fat.

I found it hard, and didn't know what to do to change. Sometimes I felt that I should accept this illness, and just live with it, but that was not healthy and it's an unhappy way to live my life; but I didn't know how to change or get myself better. I had tried everything and just needed to take one day at a time.

HURTING

49. Mum's Special Birthday

This year mum had a special birthday on the 25th January. I was thinking about taking her to a Caribbean restaurant and asking just her close family to attend. So I asked my cousin Rachel, one of my mum's close nieces, and my brother. They said it was a good idea, but didn't know whether there was wheelchair access. I then asked Kirsty, mum's closest niece, and she suggested that I look into having a party for mum instead. I said that would be a very good idea. I spoke to Mark about it again and he agreed. I started to make plans for mum's surprise 80th birthday party. I had just over 3 weeks to plan this, so I had to start moving really fast.

Once I had started it all went smoothly. I asked our pastor about having it at the church, and he said that it would be fine. He also said that we could have it on the Sunday evening, and they wouldn't have an evening service on that night. He said this because mum was such a wonderful member of the church, and she had worked so hard when she was well; she deserved it, and everyone could attend. I then thought that this was going to be a big party. I invited mum's brother who lived in Huddersfield, four of our neighbours who had known mum for the last 30 years, all her nieces, and most of her nephews, great-nieces and nephews, and all her church friends. I spoke to the staff at the nursing home and they were excited about it too. My brother Mark was very helpful - he told me to speak to one of the church members who was a very good caterer; she would be able to organise the food and make the cake etc.

The church friend did indeed organise everything, even things I had not thought of. She talked to me about it and then went away and arranged it. I sorted mum's clothes out, and bought her a lovely pink dress; (pink was mum's favourite colour.) I wanted it to be a surprise party, and when mum asked me about the party I said "What party? I am not organising a party," and then changed the subject quickly. I am not sure mum was totally convinced that nothing was going on.

On the day itself, I ordered some flowers to be delivered to the nursing home sometime during the day. I had booked the day off work and also bought her a present, because I still wanted her to think that nothing special was going on. I brought my uncle and aunty down to the nursing home, and mum started to ask about her party, "Uno having a party, ain't it!" she said in her patois accent. We all just said we didn't know anything about it, and changed the subject quickly!

On the day of the party I had Sean, Jane and Paul with me and we rushed around, making the church hall ready and decorating it. When I left the hall I came home to check the answer machine, just to check that nobody had left a message to ask where the hall was. There was a message from the nursing home, however, to say that Mum wasn't well and she had had to be taken to hospital. I was very upset and worried and I rushed over to the hospital to see what was wrong. When I got there mum was sitting up; I asked her what was wrong, and she said her chest was hurting. The doctor said that mum had to stay in hospital overnight for observations. I was really upset and worried for mum, and I was also very worried about the party because I didn't know what to do. Everyone told me not to worry, and we would wait until the morning to sort it out.

I just went home and cried. I really wanted mum to have a special day because she deserved it. I went back to the hospital and spent most of the night with her; she was alright in herself, but they had to monitor her because of the chest pains. I left the hospital that night at 1a.m, and when I went back at 8.00a.m in the morning to see how mum was, the nurse said that she had had a good night's rest, and the doctors would see her later on in the morning.

I spoke to Kirsty who told me not to worry about anything, for mum could have her party later, and she would help. The doctor came to see mum and checked her over and said she was fine. They organised transport to get her back to the Home. Whilst Kirsty and I were helping her to dress, ready to go back to the home, mum was talking to her, saying that she thought she had had a bit of indigestion which amused us. She still had no idea what was coming, so it was going to be a bit of a surprise for her.

50. The Party

The taxi came, and we soon arrived back at the nursing home. The nursing staff were very good, and helped mum get ready for the party. Kirsty did mum's hair; she helped a lot, encouraged me, and was positive about the party. I really appreciated it, especially because she was so calm.

To my surprise everything ran nearly on time. The party was supposed to start at 6.00 pm and we got there at 6.30p.m, which was excellent timing. When mum arrived, everyone clapped. She was a bit surprised to see her brother, her cousin from Huddersfield, one of dad's cousins from Dudley, and all her neighbours. There were a lot of church brothers and sisters, former ones and present ones, and most of her family also made it to the party. I could tell mum really enjoyed it. There were speeches from family members and close friends, and Mark and I also said something. I wrote a speech and a poem. The words of the poem were this:

M - Mother in a million and I am so proud that she is mine,
O - Overwhelming love which she shows to all who know her.
T - Her tenacity, she is not afraid, because she knows whom she believes in.
H - Humility my mum knows no pride and we honour her here.
E - Eighty years old goes with her wherever, she is so radiated.
R - Respect. My mother is a lady who commands respect because she lives to a high standard.

The word Christian is not just a title; it is a life style for her.

It was a beautiful party for my beautiful mum. When the day ended I brought my mum back to the nursing home. I stopped with her for a short time, and then I left for home. It seemed like a very long day. It was a day that I will never forget, even though it started in a worrying way; everything went to plan, and it went even better than I expected it to go. The following day, when I went to visit mum she was very tired. I put up all her birthday cards in her room and I sorted out all her presents, putting her name in her clothes before I left.

I hadn't been eating much over the last few days, for I was too busy to be worrying about food, which explains why I was so tired after the party. I had been rushing around so much that it had a knock-on effect for a few days, but mum had got the party she so deserved.

I continued to see my therapist, though I was struggling to find a way out of this. I found it hard when I was always asked whether I had made any changes or what changes could I make. I felt the changes I had made were to look at why I was afraid of food. I know that I found eating difficult, and I saw myself as being a nasty person; but in time I would hopefully change that thought. I knew it was going to take time. I had developed a real fear of eating, and I couldn't accept myself for being me. I so much wanted to move forward with this, because I hated what it had done to me.

51. The Dark Tunnel

When I go through bad times I hardly eat at all. I restrict myself to just one item, such as a small bowl of macaroni cheese, with tomato ketchup, together with one or two drinks of apple juice. I might even have some jelly babies to boost my energy levels. I would exercise as much as I could, and I would work a lot harder in classes and the gym.

The illness had become a big part of me, which is why I could not let it go- it helped me through difficult situations like illness, bereavement and death. These were hurtful situations, and because I had never been helped through these difficult times I had become emotionally trapped. I sometimes feel that people have lost patience with me thinking that I don't want to get better. I want nothing more in life than to get better, however. I know that I have to work on this deep hurt, and stop hating myself for being a bad person. I have to work it out because I do not want this illness to take my life, because I know that if I continue down this road that is what will happen.

I was getting more and more down about this problem, and also with the menopause symptoms becoming harder to cope with, having more and more hot flushes as well as the night sweats which kept me up in the night. I was gaining more and more weight, and wondered if the hospital, doctors, everyone at work and my friends thought I was making these symptoms up because I was so fat. I don't know why I was not coping with my thoughts. The only thing that seemed to help me to face each day was when I went to the gym. I had now started more classes - three classes of Body Attack every week. I loved this activity, with one hour of high impact aerobics, one hour with body weights, and I still did spinning classes too. When I went to a class or to the gym I felt better about everything. I knew that I was fat and I needed to keep my body in shape, and I felt so much better when I did a workout. When I tried to eat regularly, I just felt so dirty and disgusted with myself, thinking that I didn't deserve food. I felt that when I did try to open up and talk to anyone, they didn't really understand me, because I didn't know how to express myself or open up to anyone.

I was able to talk to mum, although her way of solving problems was by praying and telling me not to worry about everything; but at least she listened to me, and she was able to understand me better than anyone else.

When Easter came, I was really looking forward to it. I was planning to take mum to church, but mum had become ill again and they had to take her to hospital. When I got there mum was on the medical ward being assessed. Mum wasn't well- she was vomiting. When I asked one of the doctors what was wrong with her, he said they would have to monitor her for a few hours, and then send her back to the nursing home. I stayed with mum all day and she continued to be sick. In the end the doctors decided to admit her to the hospital to watch her overnight; but they still didn't know what was wrong with her. I had to see how she was overnight, thinking it could be a 24 hour bug that she had picked up.

The next day when I went to see her, she seemed a bit annoyed with me, and I couldn't work out why. She said that she wanted to get dressed and I was not helping her. I was not sure how I was supposed to help - I couldn't dress her by myself. But mum's niece was there, and we both helped her in the end. Then mum started to go on about her clothes, and I just had to go. I spoke to the nurse who said she seemed a lot better and could go back to the nursing home in the afternoon.

I went home upset; I couldn't understand why mum always seemed to take her anger out on me. I thought about this for the rest of the evening and over the Easter break. Mum had had to go through a lot of things; she had lost her husband, she was ill, and had become disabled (she had lost the use of her legs overnight, which was very hard for her). I had been there for her, and was the closest one to her; so she took all her frustrations out on me. The same for me - I would take out all my frustrations out on her. I knew mum wasn't angry with me, because a day or two later, when a very close church friend went to visit her she was saying to her that she hadn't seen me for two days and she was concerned. I thought mum needed a break from me because I was there every day for her, but when I thought about it she didn't need a break; she just needed to get her frustrations out. I knew that mum loved me because she told everyone that I was a good daughter to her, and she didn't know how she would manage without me. I would say that I loved her and she would say the same to me. I just think that we both knew how to wind each other up.

When I went to see mum she was fine with me and really happy to see me. Perhaps we both needed a break from each other. In Spring my mood seemed to get lower and lower. I just got to the stage where I had that much anger. Whenever anyone talked about their family, I got really jealous and angry. I had to get rid of the anger and block out these feelings. When I spoke to my therapist about these feelings she became concerned and spoke to the consultant who then suggested that I needed to be in hospital to get some support for a short period of time. I wasn't that keen on that idea, but I was at rock bottom and had a lot of things going round in my head.

I went into hospital for a short time. I needed to be supported because this eating disorder was just controlling me now. I couldn't even think properly, never mind eat or drink. I don't think being in hospital helped me, however. Although I needed their support, I wasn't ready. But I felt that I was ready to get the help of Cruse. I rang Cruse again, and they arranged a meeting when they could assess me again. They said they would let me know when they could see me in the next few months. I knew that I was ready now to deal with my grief, and I wasn't going to cancel the appointment this time.

After three weeks in hospital, I went home, but I didn't go straight back to work, not feeling well enough to return yet. I had time in hospital to talk more to my therapist about everything. I wasn't sleeping, drinking or eating. I guess that is why I became so confused about everything. I wanted to go to the graves, though I wasn't sure why. Maybe I needed to be close to dad and George, or I needed to just get them out of my head. So on the 5th July 2006 I visited dad's grave, and wrote in my diary. *"I am with dad in a way. I'm at his grave trying to remember happier times; still feeling numb, pain and a great loss. I am just wishing I had done more for dad when he was around. I told him how much he meant to me."* Maybe if I hadn't started this stupid diet I would have been able to feel something, and I would be able to grieve for my dad. After visiting dad's grave I went over to visit George's grave. I wrote: *"I feel so sad here. It just feels so horrible sitting by George's grave; I wish I was dreaming and that I was not here. I know if he was still around he would have been full of advice for me and mum. Even when he would give me advice and I didn't listen he would never stop. I remember his laugh and smile; he was so intelligent. George's life was cut short. I have lost two people that I loved and cared for. This pain is too hard to bear."*

I needed to go to the graves because I needed to start to heal and I wanted to see if it would help me. When I went into hospital, friends and family couldn't understand why I didn't answer their calls. That is how I coped when I got very stressed and down; it was not that I was ignoring them, or that I didn't want to know. It is just the way I coped when I was down. I could not explain myself if they asked me. I would say I was fine and when I tried to explain myself I felt people didn't understand. I stayed away for my birthday in October, and around the time of the 3rd anniversary of George's death (the 16th), I booked a week's holiday in Cyprus.

I returned to work at the end of summer. I had been looking forward to the new term while I was away in hospital. I still kept in touch with mum and rang her every day. My cousin Rachel used to visit her when she lived at home and in the old nursing home.

I settled back into work again, meeting new children and parents, and building relationships with the children; helping them to get used to the nursery. Most of the children seemed to settle into the nursery very well, and I was alright when I settled back into work again.

I was happy to see how well mum was doing in the nursing

home. Everything was so much better at this nursing home. The nurses were very helpful and friendly, and always helped me whenever I wanted a taxi to take my mum out; I was really grateful for their help. There were days when mum didn't want to be there, and wanted to come home, but she said she was much happier there; she enjoyed some of the activities, such as their exercise morning. She showed me how she exercised by stretching her hands up and down in the air. This was quite funny and made us both laugh.

I was also introduced to the vicar who visited the Home every week to see mum. The vicar prayed and celebrated the Lord's Supper with mum every week, which she really enjoyed, for it gave her a lot of spiritual help and comfort.

52. Cruse Work

At the beginning of the Autumn, I got a letter from Cruse to start my counselling sessions. I was very nervous about it, but I wanted to start because I knew it was something that I had to deal with. I had avoided it and not really tried to talk about the subject, mainly because there was no-one who would talk about it with me.

The first session I had was just an introduction. I talked about dad and George and their deaths and how I felt about it all. The session was very hard, because it was something I had never done before. It was totally different from the kind of work I did at the hospital. I agreed that we would see each other regularly every week. We decided that we would start focusing on my dad's death.

I felt alright about this, though I knew that it was going to be hard work. I would just have to see how it went. I was still seeing my therapist at the hospital, but when I went to see her again, she told me that she was leaving the hospital because she had found another job. I was sad about this, because I had done a lot of positive work with her, looking and thinking about my future which I found very useful, though I didn't start to eat the six meals a day which was what the hospital wanted. I continued to struggle with food, just eating enough to survive on each day; food had become my enemy.

My second appointment with Cruse was harder than the first one. We talked about dad, and it was nice talking about how special he had been to me, and how important he had been in my life. We didn't talk about George, as she felt it best to deal with dad's death first. I was alright with that; whichever way we dealt with it was going to be very hard for me.

I realised that I should have gone to Cruse after Dad's death. Perhaps if I had done so, I wouldn't have developed the eating disorder, or it would have been caught earlier.

I had my usual appointment with my hospital therapist

also. I was beginning to find this hard, trying to work both with my illness and my bereavement.

All this was really difficult, and it was beginning to really upset me. I felt I needed to cry to let everything out, but I find showing my emotions really difficult. I always put on a brave face, because that is the way I have been since I was a child, it is part of Jamaican Culture. I find it very hard to cry, and when I do cry I never stop; instead I feel weak and I cannot control myself. So I have to hold it together instead.

I had my last appointment with my therapist before I was off on annual leave. I wanted to buy her a card to thank her, so in the morning I went to the gym to do my workout and later I went to the shops to buy a card. When I was in one shop I had a message on my phone to say my mum was ill and had been taken to hospital again. The message was from my brother. They had contacted him because they hadn't got my new mobile number (I had forgotten to give it them); they had also left a message on my home phone. I rang the Home back straightaway. They said that mum was ill - she was in hospital and they wanted to talk to me.

53. My Precious Mum

I was confused by this message and didn't know what to do, so I made my way to my hospital appointment to say goodbye to my therapist and to give her the card. First I tried to ring the hospital twice, but couldn't get through. When I finally got through, I said that I would be there within the hour. I asked about mum, and they said she couldn't say anything. I was really panicking and was very worried. I went to my therapist, gave her the card and explained what was happening, then thanked her and left.

I got to the hospital within the hour, but mum was on the ward and the doctors were still with her as were the staff from the nursing home. I asked the nursing home staff member what was wrong with mum, and she said she had become very unwell. When I had visited her the day before with Kirsty, I noticed that her legs were very swollen. I mentioned it to the nursing staff, and they said they would have a look at it.

When I was able to see mum she was lying on the bed with an oxygen mask on. They were also monitoring her blood pressure, pulse and heart rate. I saw the doctor who gave me some very shocking news, namely that mum was very ill and wouldn't make it through the night.

I just broke down; I thought I couldn't be hearing this right. The nurse from the nursing home was very good, and stayed with me. I didn't know what to do, so I rang Mark and he said he would be there as soon as he could. The nurse stayed with me until he arrived. I also rang Kirsty to let her know too.

I sat beside my mum in a daze. Before I knew it, there were a lot of people at the hospital. Most of the family was there. I just didn't know what to do or say to anyone. The doctor told us they didn't expect mum to make it; they thought that she had had a stroke and that her kidneys weren't working, but they didn't really say what was wrong with her. This just made it more confusing for me and everyone else. I had already said to myself that I was going to stay at the hospital all night; I didn't want to leave her.

We all stayed with mum until about 9.00 pm, when most of the family left, saying they would be back in the morning and to ring if there was any change. At about 10.00pm Mum woke up, and to our delight opened her eyes as if she had woken after a long sleep. We stayed all night with her; she was still very ill, but was responding and talking to us. I left the hospital at 4.00am; Kirsty said I could stay with her, so I drove to her house and stayed the night.

Next morning I rang work to let them know what was happening, and said that I wouldn't be in the next day. I went straight to the hospital to see mum, who was sitting up and trying to have a drink. She was responding well, and was hoping for some good news from the doctors. When the doctors came onto the ward, they said she was still very ill, with lots of complications. I got the feeling they didn't really know what was wrong with her, which I found very frustrating and not very reassuring.

For three days mum didn't really make any progress; she had to be on a drip which made her bloated, and nothing really improved. I went back to work for two days. I left work on the Friday evening and went to the hospital, to be told by the nurse that she wasn't going to make it. That night all her nieces were there, and a friend, and we all prayed and sang for most of the night - it was so lovely. They left early in the morning, and there was a lovely moment when I sang with mum and she turned to me with a lovely smile. We sang for most of the morning, but mum started to get low in the afternoon.

They said mum wouldn't last another day, she was so poorly. We contacted as many of the family as we could. My uncle from Huddersfield arrived on Sunday afternoon, and mum's nephews and other family came also. Because most of the family had been with mum on Friday night, I thought I would stay with Mum on the Saturday night. I went to Kirsty's house to rest, while Mark stayed at the hospital. He had driven from Huddersfield to get our uncle, so he was really tired, and he had to go to work in the morning.

I went to the hospital at midnight. Mark left and I stayed all night. I read mum her favourite psalm, Psalm 23, and just kept talking to her. Psalm 23 reads:

1. The Lord is my shepherd; I shall not want.
2. He maketh me to lie down in green pastures; he leadeth me beside the still waters.
3. He restoreth my soul; he leadeth me in the paths of

righteousness for his name's sake.

4. Yea, though I walk through the valley of the shadow of death; I will fear no evil for thou art with me thy rod and thy staff they comfort me.
5. Thou prepares a table before me in the presence of mine enemies, thou anointest my heart with oil my cup runneth over.
6. Surely goodness and mercy shall follow me all the days of my life, and I will dwell in the house of the LORD forever.

I stroked her head and kissed her. It was a long night. She was not able to respond to me anymore. It was like when dad passed away, for she was lying on the bed unconscious. The nurse came in to wash her mouth out and check up on her. In the back of my head I thought "Come on, mum, make it through the night, to prove the doctors wrong and get better." I was hoping and praying.

At about 6.00 a.m. on the 1st October 2006 my wonderful precious mum passed away. She took a few deep breaths and then she was gone; at first I thought she was sleeping, so I called the nurse. She said she was gone, and I tried to phone my brother but I couldn't get through. Instead I phoned my cousins, and then went back to mum. The doctor checked her over, listened to her chest, and confirmed that she had indeed gone. I rang my cousin again, then I rang my brother and told him. He said he was on his way. I was numb and shocked. I kept walking in and out of the ward, looking at mum, and not really believing that she had gone.

When my brother arrived he collected the papers the nurse gave him and we left. I couldn't stay in the ward looking at my mum lying there. I went home, and my brother came to the house for a while. I had to get out, so I went for a drive. Kirsty rang, saying that her sisters were all at the hospital - they wanted to say goodbye to mum. Kirsty said I should go to her house, and I said I would meet her later. The whole day was very hard; I had many phone calls from friends and family, sending their regards. I felt numb and I didn't know how I would get through the loss of mum. I was just lost.

Over the next few days the hours were filled with funeral arrangements - going to the undertakers, and organising mum's service. It was really sad, for there were arguments about silly things because everyone was sad and angry and this is how it came out. I was still feeling really lost at times; I didn't know what to do or who to talk to, but I wanted to tell someone how I was feeling.

A week after mum had died I was supposed to be going out to sort out the flowers with my cousins. I couldn't bear to go out. When a friend rang I just burst into tears and I couldn't stop. This was the first time since mum had died that I had cried so much. I couldn't hold it in any longer. I had lost my best friend, someone whom I loved and respected; she was the only one who really understood me. It was hard to think about the future now, but I knew that somehow I had to go on. It was a case of how I was going to manage. I did put on a brave face for the rest of the day and through the next week, because I had to hold it together. I wanted mum to have a lovely funeral service with everything going well.

During the week, I didn't have any energy to exercise, because I wasn't eating very much - I was too busy running around trying to organise the funeral arrangements. I was just eating in the evening, and maybe I would have a drink with it. I found not drinking very easy.

The week of mum's funeral was very busy with lots of things to do and think about. We planned to give tributes, and I wanted to do one. I worked on a tribute with a close friend who helped me. I had a lot of phone calls, which was nice, though I didn't know what to do with people's kind words because whatever they said, they couldn't take away how I was feeling. I have learnt from previous bereavements that during this stage of bereavement nothing seems real; it is all like a dream and because I was so numb it felt as if mum hadn't really died, but was still in the nursing home. It just didn't seem real.

We had to have mum's funeral clothes made. The lady who made mum's dress did a good job in a very short time; she worked really hard and finished it in two days.

I didn't want to go and see mum in the funeral home. I didn't want to see her like that - maybe there was a part of me that didn't want to accept that she was gone. The funeral was on the 13th October 2006 (my birthday.) I didn't mind it being on that day as it was spoiled anyway. George had died on 16th October, three years earlier. My birthday was now between two bereavements so it will never be celebrated the same way again. Anyway the day before the funeral I had to take the lady who made mum's dress and my auntie to the funeral home so they could dress mum; I had to wait for them outside while they dressed her. I couldn't help them, for I would have been in pieces.

I sat outside and waited for them to finish. When they had finished, my auntie asked me if I wanted to go in to see mum. I said no. My auntie tried to get me to go in, and they both said she looked lovely. I said no way could I face up to doing it. When we finished at the funeral home I came home. I was expecting a lot of people that evening to visit the house. A lot of church members were coming round after they had been to the church where mum's service was going to be held. I was expecting other family members to come to the house also, so it was going to be busy. I had a house full of visitors that night, which was good because I didn't have much time to think about the next day.

On the day of the funeral I woke early and I got everything together. Jane had slept over with me, which was nice. The flowers arrived very early, which was good. The flowers were beautiful, and had been left in the front garden. Kelly and the girls arrived at the house early that morning too. At about 9.30 a.m. Mark rang me to tell me that the undertakers were on their way. We went to wait in the front of the house. When the cars arrived and I saw the coffin my heart sank, because I knew now that this was final. This is the final day for my mum, it was not a dream.

The church service went very well and all the tributes were lovely. Sandra and Sean read a scripture, and Jane sang a lovely song. My tribute is as follows –

I just want to talk to you about my mum, to tell you how special she was to me. I was glad that I had the opportunity to tell her this on her 80th birthday whilst she herself could hear me. My mum was a strong woman of faith, she had a faith that I have admired and always will admire. For my mum, God was the centre of her life; she not only loved God, but she also had an unwavering love for her immediate, extended, and church family *and friends. My mum had a hope that was firm and I have heard that love casts away fear, and I also believe that, because my mum was fearless. I remember as a child my mum was always singing around the house; one of the songs I remember was Precious Jesus Hold My Hand. I truly believe that she had a firm belief that he was holding her hand. Her dedication to her husband had her caring for him whilst she herself was unwell. I think my mum was unwell for most of her life, yet she was blessed with eight decades. It is my belief that this was because of her relationship with God. My mum has left me physically now. I've had forty precious years with my mum, and as our lives were so intertwined she will forever hold a special place in my heart. Today is very difficult for me, but I am comforted that because of her faith and conduct she is resting peacefully with her Lord.*

There were other tributes from church friends, and the church choir sang. Mark read the eulogy. After the service we all went to the cemetery, and mum was buried next to dad, so they were together again, with George also buried close by. During the service at the graveside I found it very hard, watching mum being buried - it was so final.

We went to the hall for the reception afterwards. I could have quite easily gone home, for I was wondering how I was going to live without mum. The next few weeks I tried hard to move on and not become too depressed. Most of all I didn't want to give up on life, and so I made a decision to go back to work the next week. I didn't want to sit at home on my own for too long. It was difficult when I went back to work, but I got through the day. I returned to the gym, and to my three classes. I knew that I needed to be out of the house, and to be active, to take my mind off things.

I hardly ate anything; I hadn't been eating or drinking from the moment that mum became ill. When mum was in hospital, I was having two drinks and a slice of toast most days. When I stayed at Kirsty's house, after mum passed away, she was really good and encouraged me to eat a bit more. It was hard, but I knew I was going to be really busy during the daytime, and I knew I was going to burn off whatever I ate.

54. Getting Away

I went to Cyprus at the end of October. I had originally booked this holiday in the summer for the beginning of October, but I'd had to cancel it because of mum's death, and then rebook it later. I thought it would be good for me to get away because of what had happened, but I didn't enjoy the holiday at all.

The weather was bad, and my hotel, outside Larneca, was miles away from everything. The only good thing was that it had a gym and I went to it every day. I did meet a nice person who picked me up one day and took me for a drink. I went on day trips too. I think that it was just too soon after mum's death, for I just couldn't stop thinking about what had happened.

The holiday was only for one week. When I returned, I immediately went back to work, but I felt terrible - I missed my mum so much. Although she had lived in the nursing home, I visited her 4-5 times during the week and every weekend. When I had plans to do things with friends, I used to sort everything for mum first, and now she was no longer there. I didn't want to be here anymore either, having lost my three loved ones.

I had rung Cruse to let them know about mum, and I arranged to see someone after my holiday. The first appointment after mum's death was really difficult, because I talked about what had happened in the hospital when mum had passed away, and we also talked about the funeral. It was hard. I thought that it would take a long time for me to settle into the sessions, but I had to try even though I felt so down.

55. Hurting Myself

I also started to see another therapist at the hospital - this was the fourth now. I just wanted to see someone at the hospital because I felt so down about everything, and I knew my eating disorder was at a low point. I thought I needed the support. I was really finding it hard because Christmas was coming nearer and I was not coping at all, just thinking about dad, George and mum. The thing about Christmas which makes it harder is that it is all about families, and most of my family were dead. It was hard to think about Christmas and not think about them. It would be my first Christmas without mum. Every time I heard the word "Christmas" I physically wanted to hurt myself - it just felt bad. I got so desperate that I used pain-killers to numb the pain and make me feel better. The use of the pain-killers became out of control, though I didn't want to kill myself. I was just in so much pain; I needed something to take the pain away.

My thoughts were always on my mum, dad and George; a part of me wanted to be with them. I thought that wherever they were was a better place than where I was at the moment. My eating was really bad; I would have 3 or 4 fish fingers with bread, 2 sports drinks and usually sweets to keep my energy levels up. I needed this in order to do my exercise regime of 16 hours a week. That's the only real reason I ate, so that I had enough energy to exercise. My friends said I should just go to other family members, but I don't think that they realised how bad I was feeling. I didn't want to be here; I wasn't living, I was just existing. I was empty, I was battered and bruised, and it felt that my heart had been ripped out. I couldn't go on; everything had got really bad, and just before Christmas I was admitted to hospital.

I spent a few days in hospital to settle down, and then returned home before Christmas. I spent the day with my cousin. I don't think my family ever understood how I felt, not seeing how the eating disorder helped me when I lost loved ones. As a result I did not need to try hard and explain to anyone how I felt. But on Christmas Day, remembering some of the things Cruse had said, I planned to do something special to remember loved ones.

They said I could ring the helpline if I wanted to talk. I had leave to go home, but I went back to hospital just before the New Year and spent New Year's Day in hospital. I had to try my best to look forward to the New Year, hoping to have a chance to work on my eating disorder and make a fresh start.

At the Eating Disorder Unit the routine was the same: meal times, sitting time, weight days and ward rounds. I settled down on the ward, but for one or two days I felt restricted and restless. As an in-patient all you seem to do is eat and sit around all day, which made me irritable and restless. I just couldn't cope in there, but I did my best to follow the programme and be patient. I knew that now was the best time to start concentrating on myself, because I didn't have anyone or anything else to worry about.

One morning I was upset at the start of the day. After the breakfast sitting time, which is one hour, I was called for a therapy session. I really needed to talk that morning. I started to talk to the therapist, but we soon had to leave the room because it was snack time. My therapist said that she would see me after the snack, which was very frustrating.

There was a lot going on in my head. It was only three months since mum had died. My head was telling me that I was too fat and that if I kept eating like that I would be even fatter. I needed to go to the gym and also to starve myself. I also think I still wanted to be with my mum; it was so hard that morning. I got so frustrated with everything that I just had to leave there. I knew it wasn't a sensible thing to do; I just didn't see the point of staying there, putting on 6 stones without being able to sort out my emotional side.

NEW START

56. Life without Mum

Maybe it was too soon after my mum's death to talk about it. It all comes down to me not talking about my feelings and thoughts. Maybe that has been my problem with this illness from day one. I was signed off work by my GP, as I wasn't able to concentrate on anything for any length of time.

I was now at a very low point. I started to think that I ought to do what I felt that I did best, which was to restrict my eating and increase exercise. I had to do more exercise; sometimes by the end of the week I had done up to 21 hours of exercise so I could make myself disappear. I wasn't eating until the evening. I found everything hard. I had all this time on my hands, because I wasn't going to see mum anymore and I suddenly began to feel very lonely and down. I was still living in the family home, but I couldn't make it feel like home a lot of the time. I felt really depressed in the house, because I couldn't get away from the memories, and I was missing mum, dad and George so much.

Sometimes when sitting in the house I would think about mum and all the times we had had together, and how busy she used to be around the house. I would find it really hard to deal with these thoughts, and I wanted to be away from them by going to the gym, anywhere to get away from them.

I was still seeing the therapist at the hospital, and also going to Cruse. I found going there really helpful, for the lady I was seeing was really good and I could open up to her and tell her how I was feeling. She thought I had had a lot of bereavement in a short space of time. The problem was that I couldn't talk about anything to anyone because all my emotions were in a bottle and it was shut; it was very difficult for anyone to open it because it was closed so tightly, and it was taking lots of people to open it.

Whilst I was off work, many of my close friends rang to offer me support, but I could see it was a strain for them because I closed down and shut everyone out; that is how I dealt with things. I was also referred to Occupational Health for help but I knew that in the end I had to get to a stage where I could help myself. I had to keep going because I couldn't feel any more depressed than I did. I knew if I kept going I would see some light at the end of the tunnel. The thing that kept me going was my mum, because I thought about her and all the different situations and illnesses she had had, and yet she had never given up. She fought on with life until the very end, and her faith in God will always live on in my memories.

As I began to think more clearly, I began to feel that a fresh start was what I needed. I thought it would help at work to start eating, because nobody would know I had an eating disorder so I wouldn't be self-conscious when I started eating with them. Also moving away from home would help me - not being surrounded with memories. I really wanted to make a fresh start.

My sessions at Cruse were really helping me, for I was talking about my mum and my dad too. The therapist helped me to realise that it was important to talk about them and to remember them and that there is no time limit on how long anyone is supposed to grieve. I struggled with my feelings of being empty and lost. I looked at photos of mum all the time, because I missed her so much. I thought I was not dealing with things very well, but Cruse made me realise that grieving was normal. They also began to understand how I had become so dependent on my eating disorder.

After being off work for a few months, my GP thought that I was well enough to return to work, but in a new setting. I was signed back on, which pleased me, for I felt I was ready to go back to work now. I had done a lot of hard work with Cruse. The best thing now was to get back into a normal routine.

When I returned to work, I was told that because I had been seen by Occupational Health I would have to wait until they saw me again before I could return to work, so I had to go back home again. I was so fed up, but I had to stay positive. I started to think about going on holiday to Canada. I contacted the cousin in Canada whom I visited few years ago. I had really enjoyed myself there and had even thought about living there. I began to think about that possibility again because I really did love it in Canada. A new start over there was worth thinking about.

I knew it would take a long time before I was seen by Occupational Health, so I had to keep myself as busy as I could; I didn't want to become depressed as I did before Christmas. My eating disorder was no better and I was still struggling, unable to cope with meals - all I would eat was sandwiches, pasta and bits of salad, sweetcorn and something sweet to keep my blood sugars high. When I went to the leisure centre to do exercise it was good, because I had lots of people to talk to who didn't know anything about me. I somehow felt relaxed and able to be myself around them. We all had something in common, for we all loved to be in the gym or in an exercise class.

One of my friends at work had been very supportive during my mum's illness, and also when she had passed away. Sheena was a tower of strength, often ringing me to find out how I was. Sometimes she invited me to her house for the afternoon, and we often went to the cinema together too. I could share a lot of my thoughts with her and I knew she would be honest and open with me. I always tried to change for other people around me - I wanted to get better to make everyone happy. When it didn't work, I felt I was letting everyone down - my friends would be very disappointed and annoyed because I didn't eat. I know a lot of my friends and family have been very upset with me and annoyed because I haven't eaten a meal or solved this problem. If only it was as easy as that, I would have been better by now. I think that most of my friends still think that I don't try; they don't realise the daily battle that goes on in my head every day.

57. Moving to Canada
- would I be better off?

My cousin in Canada rang me and said that I could stay with her for a holiday. I was so happy and pleased; I couldn't wait to book my holiday, and I booked it for the beginning of July; I was really looking forward to going again. My cousin told me that she had now moved house, which made me more excited. I was going to look at the possibility of work and a fresh start over there. When I saw my therapist at the hospital I talked to her about my future plans. She asked me why I wanted to make such a big decision. I said that since my mum had died I didn't think I had a future here anymore. I was finding it hard to live on, for I missed my mum so much, and there was a big hole in my life. I was now living around memories of dad, George and mum, and I was not handling it at all well. At least if I moved I could look to the future and become positive.

My therapist thought it was too big a decision to make, and advised me to be patient, because it had only been 7 months since mum had died. But I was still really grieving and needed a fresh start.

When I went for my Occupational Health appointment, I went through everything about my health and about work. They listened and they asked a lot of questions. They then asked if I would write for a report from my consultant. I was happy for that to happen. They would see me when the report was sent back to them. I guessed that I would have to wait until that happened before I went back to work. Meanwhile I had my holiday in Canada to look forward to. I had to book my annual leave from work before I went, so I knew my holiday was near once I had done that.

I was thinking like this: "I really wish I could get on with my life. I am now finding it really hard and really stressful being stuck with this problem. I have now forgotten what it feels like to be well, because every day I feel tired, confused and unwell. I find it hard to enjoy food. In fact I stopped enjoying food many years ago; whenever I eat I think about my next workout and how I have to work out harder and longer. If I don't get to the gym, I feel fat and lazy and I cannot eat anything for the whole day because I am too fat to be eating and not exercising enough. I don't know why I ever wanted to go on a diet in the first place; I should have stayed how I was - overweight. I don't even feel that I have lost any weight, still being overweight and out of shape."

I have had a lot of bad days in the last 7 months since mum died. I tried hard to work through the way I was feeling; the good thing about it was that at least I was not sitting around the house. I was out exercising most of the time and keeping myself busy. I also had my hospital appointments and I saw Cruse every week to work through all this grief bottled up inside. I had my appointment with my consultant before I went on my holiday, and I talked through my plans for Canada and discussed the report that Occupational Health wanted him to do for me.

My appointment with my consultant went alright. I told him how I was doing with my eating disorder. I said that I wasn't really coping with things at the moment. He suggested ways of trying to cope. I talked about Canada and how I felt about making a fresh start. He also said it was too early to be making a big decision like that. I said I needed to do something different because I felt that I was stuck at the moment. My holiday was only a week away and I was really looking forward to it.

When the day came I had an early start, catching the coach to the airport. The flight to Montreal was a long one, but it was really relaxing and I was really looking forward to seeing my cousin Shanice. She met me at the airport with her husband. It felt so good to be out of England and away from home. I felt relaxed and not stressed. We all had a good chat in the car on the way to my cousin's house. The house was on a nice quiet estate; it was quite big and had a large living room.

The kitchen area was not that large but it was nice; the basement area was big with another living room and laundry room; upstairs there were three bedrooms and a bathroom; they also had a downstairs toilet. There was a small garden with a pool in it, and a nice front garden. My cousin made me feel at home and showed me to my room. Whilst I was unpacking the kids came home; they had finished their summer day camps. I went to meet them - two lovely kids. I had dinner with them, then I had a really early night – first a shower, then to bed at 8.30 pm. I was so tired I went to sleep straightaway.

There was so much I wanted to see while I was there, for I wanted to see all the sights. My cousin took me to the local bus stop and showed me which bus would take me to the centre of Montreal and how to get to the tube station. The first two days I just got used to the time change and then I tried to do as much as possible. In Montreal the shopping mall was just "something else". There is an underground shopping centre that goes on for miles, with six floors all together. I also went to the Olympic Park where Canada held the Winter Olympics in 1974. I went for a tour around the park and I visited the beautiful and relaxing Botanic gardens.

There was a fantastic carnival whilst I was there, with beautiful coloured costumes. The parade was great - I had never been to a carnival before - and there was an Arts festival on for a week, with a lot of bands and acts to see. I went to the Arts festival most days whilst it was on - what with walking and sightseeing I was out all day.

My cousin and her husband were at work for most of the day, but I was very independent and quite happy to entertain myself. I did have some time with my cousin when she wasn't at work, and I talked to her about living in Canada. She said it would be possible. The only disadvantage about living in Montreal was that they were all French-speaking as French was their first language. If I wanted to work in schools I would have to speak the language. This was a bit disappointing, but it was something I didn't want to dismiss. I would look at it more in the future, or look into going to Toronto where there were more English speakers.

I decided to visit Toronto next time. I had a fantastic time in Canada. I found a gym and went there most days; I wasn't looking for a gym, but I passed one on my way home. I went in and paid to use it. I always worry about gaining weight and when I don't exercise I feel lazy. Even though I was walking for miles every day I tried my best to eat at my cousin's house. She said that she didn't know how I survived. I also did family things with them all, like shopping, and the cinema; we also had a family day in on one of their bank holidays which was nice. It was great for me just to be around people and have people to talk to, even though I just wanted to sit and read a book and let my cousin and her husband have time together, because they had been at work all day. At least I was with people - which I needed ever since my dad died.

58. Returning To Work

I didn't really want to leave Canada or leave my cousin because I'd had a great time there and felt relaxed. I still thought about what had happened to mum and everything I had to deal with when I returned home, but it all seemed to be a million miles away. The holiday was now over, however, and I had to face life at home again.

When I returned home I received a letter from Occupational Health with an appointment to see them. I thought they had got my letter, or the report from my consultant, and that I would be back to work by the end of the summer. Whilst I was waiting for the appointment I had my weekly session with Cruse, and told them how I was feeling since I had returned from my holiday. I said that I felt that I had to be away from Birmingham because of all the memories. My counsellor reminded me that wherever I went I would still have memories of mum, dad and George, because they were all part of me and leaving would not take the memories away.

After this appointment I went away and thought about what the counsellor had said. Whether I lived in Birmingham, Canada, America or anywhere, I would still have memories of birthdays and Christmas and family events. You always think about them sometime; often I would think to myself "I wonder what mum would think, looking at my nieces and nephews." I often thought how proud mum and dad would be of them. Maybe it's not about where I was to live after all. I had to continue with my work with Cruse since it was helping me a bit in dealing with my loss, but I was working through several bereavements, not just one.

When I went to see Occupational Health they went through the report from my consultant: -

Miss Foster continues to suffer from a clinical, significant eating disorder. Over time the pattern has evolved into a picture where she will restrict her dietary (and fluid) intake and episodically binge eating. An additional pathological means of weight control which Miss Foster employs is to exercise to an excessive degree as a way of burning energy. At present there is little structure to her pattern of eating.

In addition to her eating problems she has suffered from broader emotional difficulties including depressed moods. I understand that she is not currently in contact with general psychiatric services but was assessed in general psychiatry in February 2007. At that time she was assessed as being intact.

Miss Foster was assessed in Eating Disorders Services in 1996. At the time her weight put her within the normal range for body mass index. She was first seen by me personally in November1998. At that time she did not meet full syndrome criteria for a clinical eating disorder but had some of the features of anorexia nervosa. She was dissatisfied with her body and had a morbid fear of weight gain. At the time she was misusing laxatives and diuretics but did not report binge eating (in the objective sense of the term).

Her eating problems date back to 1995. The onset of her eating difficulties came after the death of her father.

A number of different treatment options have been offered during the course of Miss Foster's illness. She has had a number of admissions both to in-patient and day-patient care. She has been treated with various forms of psychotherapy in both group and individual format and has also engaged in counselling. She has, as mentioned above, also input from the Local Mental Health Team. Their input is largely focused upon intervention for her depression and bereavement. Her treatment for depression has included anti-depressant medication.

With regard to prognosis, factors which would have a bearing are the length of her history and her level of engagement in treatment. Additionally, her co-morbid depression and bereavement issues will be factors as will her pre-morbid level of adjustment. Whilst it is not possible on the basis of this information to give an accurate prognosis I would anticipate that

Miss Foster will continue to experience significant eating problems in the short to medium term. To give an indicative time scale, I would suggest that in the space of the next six months it is unlikely that she will be symptom-free.

The consultant said that I needed set times to have a drink and a room where I could go to do so. I knew that this would be difficult if I was eating on my own, but I would try it. They told me that my employers would get back in touch with me and give me a date to return to work. I was very happy with that, but nervous about going back to work because it had been a long time - but that wasn't my fault really. When I read the report from the hospital, however, I was shocked, and it was a bit hard to take it all in. I knew that I had a problem, but when it was all set out on paper in front of me, I couldn't really hide away from it.

When I went to see my therapist on my next appointment I talked about the report with her. I didn't understand some parts of it, and she wasn't able to explain it to me, saying that I would have to discuss it with my consultant. Most people think that with an eating disorder one has to be stick-thin. I will never be that thin, because I exercise so much, so people think I have no problem. I'm making it up; they think – just pretending, because really I am overweight. This has always been something that I have really struggled with. I hate it when everyone says to me I look so well; I would prefer them to say that I look fat or that I am fat.

My manager rang me up and gave me a date to come in for a meeting. For this I would have someone like a manager to support me, so that everyone could discuss the way forward. I was very nervous about the meeting, because I wasn't sure what was going to happen. At the meeting, we all discussed a positive way forward. They were happy for me to have a ten-minute break in the morning to have a drink, and another in the afternoon, and a room to eat my lunch in. They also told me that it wasn't going to be possible for me to move; that didn't happen anymore. I hoped that a fresh start somewhere else would help me to start up a good eating pattern. I find eating with people makes me feel nervous, especially when staff know me and my struggle with food; I thought that everyone was watching me, thinking that I was greedy.

The meeting went well, and I was told that I could return to work the next day. I was happy in a way, but also worried about how it would all go. I was also informed that I would now be working in the baby unit. I have never worked with very young children, so I saw this as being very challenging but also very exciting and interesting. I just had to be positive.

I returned to work towards the end of August 2007, after being off work since December 2006. It would be hard to go back and get to know the staff again; some of them I had known for a long time, and my biggest worry was that they might expect me to be alright now. I told myself to take each day as it came and to just try and relax; and everything would go really well.

I returned to work the following day and I went into the baby unit. Everything was very strange - the whole set-up of the room, the daily routine, everything. The three staff in there really helped me, and I managed to bring in a drink and a sandwich; I did have a small drink and I ate some of my sandwich. It was very hard to do this, and I did struggle, but I managed to have something. I was very happy when I got the first day over, and the next few days continued to go quite well too. I found it very easy to settle into working in the baby room, maybe because it was the summer holidays and in the holidays we don't have as many children in the nursery - so it seemed very quiet there.

In September a few more children came in. I really enjoyed it in the baby room, and was much more relaxed, really enjoying working with the young children. I thought I would develop my career in this area because it is an important and interesting part of child development; this is the most important stage of learning. This was my best time in the nursery, and I did very well in the first few weeks with my eating, but then I started to slip back into a bad habit again. I have a battle with what my head tells me, namely that I don't need food during the day and can cope without it. I feel I am not strong enough to ignore these thoughts, and I give into them and believe them.

The eating and drinking at work lasted for about 4 weeks, but I had got used to not eating anything during the day. I really tried to get back on track with my eating. One of my friends who worked in the unit with me was very supportive; she encouraged me. She also taught me a lot about how to work with young children. When I watched her with the children, she was always on their level; she had lots of experience with this age group and had worked in the baby room for a long time. I developed a good working relationship with her. If I was unsure about something I would always ask her. I wasn't looking forward to October, however, because it was the anniversary of mum's death, and I was becoming very anxious and feeling a bit down, thinking about mum a lot. When I went to Cruse for my next session, my counsellor encouraged me to do things that I could remember mum liked. I could remember that mum liked lighting candles and visiting dad's grave. I decided to do something that would help me remember mum.

59. First Anniversary of Mum's Death

When mum's anniversary came on the 1st of October, I lit some candles around the house to remember her. I had a few phone calls from family and friends which was nice, and helped me get through the day. I feared that I would get as low as I had been last Christmas.

I also managed to get through George's third anniversary. I used to think about all three a lot – how ill they had been, and how much they had suffered, particularly in their final few days. I found this really hard.

I was told by my manager at the beginning of November 2007 that she was pleased with the way I had returned to work, and with the way I had settled into the baby unit. She said that I was interacting with the babies really well too. She also asked me if I was happy in the unit and how I felt it was going. I said I felt happy and was surprised how well I had taken to working with the younger children, and most of all, how they had taken to me so quickly. When my manager asked me if I wanted to talk about anything else, I said I was struggling with the meals. I said that this was very much up to me, for there was not a lot that my manager or anyone else could do to change this; I just had to do my best. We ended the meeting and I felt very positive and happy that everything was going so well since I had returned to work. I knew that the problems had not gone away, however, and that I still had a lot of work left to do with my eating disorder; but when things were going alright I just ignored the eating disorder. I decided that I was just fat and could continue to live like this. Only when I became ill and I could not go to work because I felt so weak, did I tell myself that I had a problem and I needed to sort it out before I became really ill.

I was really pleased with myself, being back at work, and getting a lot of job satisfaction. I was developing a good relationship with the others, communicating with each member of staff and feeling part of the team. After being off work for such a long time I didn't feel I was part of the staff team at first, but this had soon changed.

I was still finding life outside work very hard, however,

though I often had a part in my nieces' and nephews' lives, and they were a big support to me. I felt that on a lot of occasions they gave me a lot of joy and pleasure, for they are such wonderful children. It was great to be around them – after all, they were the only family that I had left. I spent a lot of time in the gym, where I felt I could meet people and talk to them. Many have become friends, and I think that this has become a good thing for me. I know when I am with them that I can just start talking and relax, being myself - they know nothing about me. That is one of the reasons why I go to the gym and do the different fitness activities which I enjoy so much. But the time of year that I don't enjoy was now approaching again, and I was going to make sure that I wasn't going to have a bad time like I did last year. I wasn't going to let it get to me.

60. Christmas

We had the usual Christmas parties at work and I joined in as much as I could, and tried to play a part in all the celebrations. I did the usual things that go towards Christmas - shopping for gifts, giving out presents etc, and I tried to plan my Christmas holiday.

I visited all my nieces and nephews and tried to spend time with them, as well as visiting my friends. I thought I could go for walks too because there would be a few days when the gym would be closed. I was going to prepare myself for Christmas better this time. I worked up to the end of term. I was dreading Christmas with all the build-up that you hear on television, and the messages from everyone that you cannot spend it on your own. Then you hear about the need to go to your family for dinner, but this illness makes me hate food, so eating is not an enjoyable occasion for me at the best of times. Because I have such a difficult time with food, I would rather avoid everyone and get together with everybody after Christmas. Also Christmas brings back so many memories for me, and I still find it a very emotional time; I still feel hurt when I think about loved ones who are not here anymore.

On Christmas Day I went to the graves very early with wreaths for everyone - dad, mum and George. I spent some time at their graves. It was nice to be there to think about them and remember the good times we had had together, and the Christmases that we all spent together. When I had visited the graves I went home again, and then took presents round to my nieces and nephews. I spent some time with them and then returned home. I had bought a few puzzles (1000 pieces) which helped me not to focus on the food, and the fact that I wasn't able to go to the gym. I was so glad when Christmas Day was over. I spent the next day, Boxing Day, at a Birmingham City football match in the afternoon, for I enjoyed going to watch football and had become a regular supporter. I loved watching football and Birmingham were a good side…they had their moments. I had a good time at the match together with Catherine, who is a season-ticket holder - she would get me in to watch a match. I always enjoyed meeting up with her and catching up with what was

159

going on in her life. We would also spend time with each other, going shopping, or maybe I would just go to her house. Catherine is a really good friend to me who has always supported me and visited me in the good times and bad; she has always tried to be there for me. When mum was alive, she and her husband went to mum's old home, the one that she moved from, to help move furniture. I really appreciated that.

The rest of the holiday went really quickly. As soon as the gym opened again I was back there, though I couldn't get back to my exercise routine. I just felt so guilty for eating so much over Christmas, and not being able to do anything energetic. I did go for a few walks, but it wasn't the same. I also went to the sales and bought a few items. On New Year's Eve, I don't know why, but I decided to go to a New Year's Eve church service.

This was a positive step for me because I worry about being around church people, and I always get very anxious about going back to the church which mum and dad used to attend - I didn't want them saying, "You look good". I see that as being really false, and that it doesn't mean anything. I wanted to go back to church to feel comfortable, and have a relationship with God. Maybe the reason I went back to my old church was to see familiar faces, and also to start a relationship with God. So I went to church in good time and sat at the back; there were a few people there already, and some of them came over to me and said hello.

The service was a baptism and soon the church was full of people. The reason why I went to church that night, I think, was because I wanted to heal inside. I had to get rid of all the hurt and sadness. I also had questions that I needed to have answered - I wanted to ask God why I was in so much pain and when was he going to take all the anger and pain away. I needed to find some peace and comfort, to see the light at the end of the tunnel. I wanted to rebuild my life again. I wanted to feel safe and secure in myself and I didn't want to feel so angry, hurt and bitter. I knew that the way I was living my life was not healthy, and I had to change to be able to start again. I also knew that a lot to people turn to God for help when they can't find the answer anywhere else. I didn't know how God would answer those questions; maybe I would have to work them out for myself.

61. New Year

New Year's Day, 1st January 2008: a positive and good way to start the new year, a new commitment, or a new start with God. I'd had a really nice holiday and was happy to go back to work to start the New Year. It was good to be back at work, seeing all the children and staff. I was looking forward to seeing the changes. Every year since I have had this illness I always see the beginning of the year as a chance to make changes, and I always hope that this year would be the year when things would really change and I would be free of this illness. I have, however, realised that it doesn't work like that, and it is not going to be as easy as that with this illness. I have realised that there are so many hurts inside that have got me into this problem; all I could do was to hope and dream that things would change in the morning. I had my first session with the therapist in the new year. I spent the session talking about how Christmas and the New Year had gone a lot better than last year. I was much happier about this and I was pleased with myself. My therapist seemed happy about this also, but when she asked me what I had eaten and if I had coped with food it made me feel really upset. Why do they have to talk about how that side is going? I often thought that they did not believe me about how much and what I ate because I was so fat. They must think I make it all up as I go along. I have to try and be more positive - it is a new year, and I won't let anything upset me.

My next appointment with my Cruse counsellor went well, with me describing how I had coped with everything during the holiday.

I explained the sort of things I did to get through Christmas, and the counsellor said that I had dealt with it well. We discussed how we should carry on with further sessions. She wanted me to focus more on my dad since we had not talked about him much. She asked me for photos of him; I said I only had 3, two of them were of mum and dad's wedding in the 60s, and the other was of dad at Mark's wedding. I had not got many pictures of my dad, and wished I had more. Sometimes when I am thinking of him I would love to look at some more; but there aren't many left of him.

I settled back into work very well, and really began to enjoy my time in the baby room. I was getting a lot of job satisfaction and was leaving work very excited about how the children were developing and growing. I had found my favourite and best age group in the whole nursery. I never thought that the baby unit would be the area which I enjoyed most.

The first six weeks of the new year went really well with work and Cruse, but I thought my hospital sessions weren't going that well. I think I should have just gone to my Cruse sessions and tried to concentrate on them - doing two sessions in one week was too much for me, and I am sure that I just made things confusing for myself. I was often talking about my issues around food with my Cruse counsellor, because I developed my eating disorder around the time of my dad's illness and death. I think the two are linked together, which makes trying to sort it out very difficult.

I had my hospital therapist appointment on 12th February 2008. While I was there my mobile phone rang, for I had forgotten to turn it off. I did not take the call as no name came up, but after the session I switched it back on - I was really worried about who had phoned me. I thought that whoever had called would ring back. On my way home the phone rang again and I pulled over to deal with it. My cousin Kirsty's name came up, but someone else spoke. They told me that a close family member had passed away in Jamaica; I could not believe what she was telling me. She said this family member had not been ill; she had always been busy, but she had died suddenly. When I had finished talking to her I couldn't carry on driving straightaway. I just sat in my car and looked around in shock. After 10 minutes I carried on driving and made my way home. When I got in, I sat on the stairs; I am not sure for how long. Mark rang me and we talked for a while. I decided to go round to the cousin's daughter's house; I felt for them because I knew how they must be feeling. I also thought that it was hard for them because they were so far away. How can it feel real for them? I spent the rest of the evening at their home.

62. Family Death

I decided that I would go to Jamaica to attend the funeral, although I knew that nothing that I said or did would make them feel better. The only comfort I could give was just to be there. The funeral was beautiful and everything went well. It was very difficult for them, but I know from experience that funerals aren't easy. I felt like I was in a different world and that it wasn't really happening. It was so tough and hard and there wasn't anything that I could say that would help them heal their pain. I stayed in Jamaica for a week altogether. The whole experience just shook me up, and left me feeling numb. I went back to work the week after I returned. I needed to get back into a routine very quickly because I had been really shocked by what had happened. I went back to my classes and gym sessions as well. I needed to blank out how much my auntie meant to me. She had supported me so well when mum was ill and when mum needed to go into a nursing home. She had been a really special person and the closest auntie to me. I realised that it is so important to tell friends and close family members how I felt about them, because we don't know how long we have got together in this world. I had to try not to let myself get too down, wanting to be able to support my cousins if I could. I wasn't sure how much support I could offer them, if any. One month after the funeral service there was a memorial service at church. The service was lovely, and it was a chance for everyone who knew her in England to say goodbye.

My cousins are very close, and I know now that the one thing that is important when you lose a parent is that you talk through those precious memories which are so important, in order to help you get through the grieving.

I began to develop really close relationships with my work colleagues, because I was feeling a lot happier and more comfortable at work. I didn't feel as tense and as unhappy as I had done in the past. I started to socialise with them, which was really nice. Sometimes on a Friday night we would decide to go to the cinema at the last minute. My friends always talked to me and supported me with my eating disorder, even though they didn't really understand it, and I don't think they ever will. I have never really told them, being scared that if they really knew how I felt, they wouldn't want to know me anymore. Also, there is that level of privacy which prevents me from wanting them to know everything about me. I don't think friends and family know much about eating disorders, because when I have been at work I have been encouraged to eat and I have had a drink; the expectation now is that I am cured, but it is not as simple as that. I always appreciate my friends for being there, and my only wish is that I could get over this problem.

In Spring 2008 my manager announced that she would be taking early retirement, which came as a bit of a shock for everyone at work. She hadn't always understood my struggles, and I know that that it must have been hard for her to know how to support me.

After my return to work after my mum's death, when I had moved to the baby unit, I had really settled down and felt much happier. This had helped me and I was able to work really well. We had regular supervisions and meetings, which had all been very positive, helping me to continue to work hard and to stay optimistic. It was hard to think about the nursery without my manager, but she knew the time was right for her to go. My worry now was how I would develop a relationship and trust with my new manager. I thought I would have to wait and see what happened. I got a bit of a surprise a couple of weeks after my manager announced she was leaving, when I had a phone call from my ex- co-ordinator, Angela, who had worked with me previously in the under-two's unit; she was great to work for - she was so much fun, and lovely with the children and parents. Out of the blue she rang me; she was still "as mad as a hatter", and was out with Rosie. I hadn't heard from Rosie for a long time, so it was great to hear from her too. Angela had emigrated to Australia and was only here for a few weeks; she wanted to pop in to see my manager before she left. I said I would see her then. I was looking forward to seeing her and to catching up with her news. When she came into work to see everyone, it was really nice for she was still the same as before. She had settled down into her new life in Australia and everything was going well in her life.

63. Summer 2008

I wish I was brave enough to make a decision like that. I know when you do something like Angela did it gives you a chance to start all over again. I seemed to be going around in circles with my treatment; the therapist said that she had to finish working with me. I said that I would never see another therapist again. I had had enough of being sent from one therapist to another, and couldn't see how this could help me or indeed anyone else. The work I had done with my previous therapist had been much more effective. I didn't think the work I had done with the present one had any impact on me at all. I was working with Cruse at the same time, though, which may not have helped.

The summer of 2008 was not a good one; my illness was at a low point, and I was really struggling. I hated my fat body - it seemed that the more exercise I took, the more I looked and felt fat. I kept wishing that I could lose weight and look like the other girls. When I looked at myself in the mirror I saw a body with big hips, fat and bulky legs, massive breasts and a fat stomach. I looked disgusting and wished I could disappear. I exercised for hours to look and feel better; I wanted to restrict my eating more every day, and I wanted to lose half a stone. I would do anything to lose some weight - even if I could tone up I would feel better. I couldn't talk to anyone about the way I was thinking because I knew they wouldn't understand. They would think I was off my head. I just had to pretend and keep my thoughts to myself.

As a result, I was exercising a lot and keeping myself busy so that I would think less about how I felt about my body. I always keep my true thoughts to myself. I knew my thoughts would be safe in my head. My plan from the beginning of the year to make a fresh start with God and to go back to church never took off. I just went on New Year's Eve and I never went back after that. In the back of my head I knew it was never going to work. I don't think I could give up my Sunday morning 'Body Attack' class to go to church. I think I will one day, but I don't know when, because I can't accept myself for who I am. I struggle to believe that God accepts me and the way I look. I spoke to the new minister at the church who had only been there for 12 months. I tried to explain how I felt since I lost members of my family. He didn't have a clue, and I could tell he didn't really understand. I know people don't understand because they see me as being fat, not someone who has an eating disorder. I wonder if anyone will see that I have a problem; maybe everyone thinks that I make it all up as I go along. I don't see myself as going back to church for a long time. I am not ready to make that change in my life yet.

The summer at work was sad because my manager had left. When we had our last session together, she wished me "all the best" and said that she was very pleased with the way things were going in the baby unit. I thanked her for all her help and support over the years. The new manager would come in at the end of summer, so it was just a case of waiting to see what she would be like. I was really nervous, mainly because when she was shown around the nursery by my old manager, I recognised her.

I had applied to her nursery for a job and she had interviewed me. When I saw her, I was apprehensive and hoped she didn't recognise me. I don't know for sure, but I found out in the next few months. Although I wasn't having any problems with my work, I was with my health. I started to have a lot of chest problems again – it was as if my heart was fluttering – that is the best way that I can describe it. It was a bit scary; I could be sitting down watching the television, then I would suddenly have a sharp pain. I went to my local A & E hospital department where they did an ECG and checked my blood pressure. They found I had an irregular heartbeat. I had to stay in hospital overnight, which turned out to be the longest night of my life. I was on a medical ward and it was awful. I must have slept for only 30 minutes that night. I was worried about what they had found out, and didn't understand what the doctors were saying to me. They told me they wanted to do more tests to find out what the cause was. I went home the next morning because I was so tired.

It was only when things like this happen that I begin to think that I needed to take this problem more seriously. When I spoke to someone about what the ECG had shown, they said that if I continued to exercise the way I did, I could end up having a heart attack. I still didn't stop; I did understand what I was being told, but I told myself that I was not that ill and it would never happen to me.

The thought of no exercise scared the life out of me. This symptom could be anything, I told myself, and was it worth worrying about? I went to see my doctor and she thought the same. I reassured myself by thinking that when I had had the test I would know more. I had my last appointment with the therapist from the hospital and then stopped, because I didn't feel it was doing me any good. Maybe I had too much anger and it was still too difficult for me to express it.

I had an appointment with my consultant in a few weeks' time and hopefully I would be able to discuss some of the issues about how I felt with him. I was now at the stage that I could say one or two things about how I felt to my friends at work. I was able to open up to Stella, whom I had known for 6 years, though it had been only over the last year that I had built up this close relationship with her. I was able to tell Stella how I really struggled with my eating, and how hard it was to stay in recovery. I also began to spend more time with her, going to the cinema, and also with Susan - I enjoyed going shopping with her although even that was hard, and it wasn't until I did things like that with my friends that I realised how my mind was set in this way of thinking. Whilst I was shopping with Susan I would go for clothes that were large sizes, because I saw myself as a large size, and felt my friends did too. I am actually half the size I thought I was, and I am sure that Susan got annoyed with me, but she never showed it. I really did enjoy being around them, but I felt that most of the time it was too much for them. That's why at times I would avoid talking to them about it; I just wanted them to accept me for who I was, and to forget about my eating disorder.

Sometimes that was not possible. If they brought up the subject, some days I could talk about it and some days I would be just too distressed to be able to say anything about it. There was also Kelly, who had supported me from the very early years with my dad's death, then with George and mum's deaths.

The new term had started, and the new manager had begun too. I tried to impress her in the first week and tried to hide the real me, for I didn't want her to be able to tell there was anything wrong. I knew that more than likely she would know about my problem; and even if she didn't know, someone would tell her. I should have just been myself from the start, however, for in the first two weeks the new manager saw all the staff and I used this as an opportunity to tell her a little about myself and my problem. I don't know if I was glad after about doing that or not. I thought that unless I moved on to where nobody knew me, there was always going to be the chance that a new person would get to hear about me. I didn't want to be known just as someone with this illness; I wanted people to see someone else, not just someone with an eating disorder.

My work with Cruse had come to an end at the beginning of September. I had done a lot of work with them and started to work on a lot of the anger which I had hidden when I buried my dad, much of which had been buried so deep down that I couldn't dig it out.

64. The illness taking over

I had an appointment with my consultant coming up, and I felt that I had to be as open and as honest as I could with him. I was talking to Claire at work about it, and she said she would go along with me. I didn't know what to do anymore - I just wanted to carry on normally and for people to accept me for the way I was. The appointment with my consultant arrived and Claire went with me. I talked about how my eating was at that moment - very poor. I started to eat salad at dinner time in the evening with a few drinks. I didn't have anything during the day. I would just have small things to eat just to keep my sugar levels from going too low. I was exercising the normal amount for me, which was about 16-18 hours a week. I also talked to him about what had happened when I went to the hospital. I talked about having treatment somewhere else, away from Birmingham, where I had no distractions. I needed to be somewhere different. My consultant started to talk to me about having treatment in the hospital again as an in-patient. At first I said I was not sure about that, but he went on to say that it was a new hospital. I had never been in there before; it would be a new environment for me, and he thought I should really think about it.

He suggested that I visited the ward to have a look around. He left it up to me to give him a ring to let him know if I was going to go into hospital. I went away and really had to decide what I wanted to do. My biggest worry was that it wouldn't work; I wouldn't cope in there. I didn't know what to do, but I knew that I had to do something to help myself. I was worried about my health and I wanted to have my heart checked also. Claire, Stella, Kelly and Susan all encouraged me to go into hospital, saying that I needed the help and that they were the best people I could get help from.

I needed to see what the ward was like, so I arranged a visit. Kelly was more than happy to visit the ward with me, so I arranged a time that would suit us both. When we were there, I thought it was alright - the good thing about it was that there was more open space on the ward to have some time out and away from everyone. I had found that in the last ward I had been on, everyone was sandwiched together and there was nowhere to go, even to have a private phone call. I also had a chat with one of the nurses about going in as an in-patient. I was so scared that it wouldn't work; the thing I feared most was that I would just get angry and walk out just like the last time. I spoke to Kelly on the way home, and she helped me look at the benefits of going into hospital. She encouraged me to be positive about it and to sort out what I thought about the ward. I was glad she had gone with me, for I was able to think about things in a positive rather than a negative way.

I took a few days to think through the advantages and disadvantages, and in the end I could clearly see that the advantages of going in as an in-patient outweighed the disadvantages. I made the phone call to the consultant to say that I would be going into hospital. It was just a case of waiting for a bed, which I knew would take a few weeks, maybe months even - I would just have to see. When I told people at work about my decision to go into hospital, everyone was glad, and my manager was really supportive also. All I had to do was to wait for a bed to become available. I wish I could say that I was positive about going into hospital as everyone else seemed to be very excited about me having the treatment. I continued my exercise routine; I couldn't stop training even though I did think that maybe I shouldn't do as much exercise, though I knew that would be very hard for me. I went to my 'Body Attack' class on a Sunday morning, and after the class I bumped into Rosie. She was going into the next class after mine; it was lovely to see her. A few days later she texted me and asked if we could get together, so we met up and went shopping at a local shopping centre. I looked forward to our trip and to spending some time with her because we hadn't got together for a long time. After we visited a few shops we stopped for a drink, which was a good thing for me to do, especially during the day. It was good to catch up, and hear about what she had been enjoying in her career. Rosie had changed her job from a career with children to the police force. I could tell she was really enjoying her new career very much. We had a drink and chatted for a while, and then we both made our way home. I thought a lot about the brave career move she had made, for I could tell she was getting so much job satisfaction from making such a big change.

Whilst I was waiting for an in-patient bed to come up I was getting more and more nervous about going into hospital. It was not as though I didn't know what would be expected of me, maybe that was the problem. I knew what to expect, and sometimes that is not a good thing; the thought of not doing any exercise was going to be very hard. There used to be a small gym at the hospital where patients could go under supervision, but that had now gone. Patients were no longer allowed to go for a walk, whereas you used to be allowed 30 minutes' walk everyday. I thought that no way could I cope on that ward. It was not worth me thinking about it; I just had to hope that it would take a long time for a bed to come up.

Mum's anniversary came along; I still did not tell anyone about it, but on the day everyone could tell there was something wrong, for I was really quiet and I just didn't say anything. This told me how much all of this was affecting me. I don't care what anyone says; when you lose a parent, brother or any close member of your family, you never get over it. I had never really grieved, which was part of my problem. I was hoping that I could continue to work on some of this in hospital for I had worked through some of my grief when I went to Cruse, and I was happy about this.

My birthday came, and I still had no phone call about an in-patient bed, which made me happy as I didn't want to have to celebrate my birthday in hospital. I went into work in the morning and had some time off in the afternoon. I spent the afternoon doing some shopping, ready for going into hospital. I also had to fit in my training routine, and I wanted to spend some time with my cousin. I had a good day. A few days later it was the anniversary of George's death; October is a month I don't look forward to at all now. No matter how hard I try to carry on and ignore it and look to the future as I am told to do, I am still going to think about and remember the loved ones who have passed away. I wish it was that easy to ignore these times.

171

LAST CHANCE FOR RECOVERY

65. Hospital In-patient again

It was now nearly the end of October, and I still hadn't had a phone call from the hospital. I knew it would be soon, because I had been on the waiting list for about a month now; it would probably come on a Wednesday, the day they did the ward rounds and discharged patients – well, that's how they used to do it the last time I was in hospital. It was indeed on Wednesday 22nd October 2008 that the call came, at 7.30pm, when I was in an exercise class. I just panicked about it, which was strange because I had been expecting the call for the last few weeks. I knew I couldn't do anything about the call until the morning; all night I kept thinking about whether I was doing the right thing.

Should I go into hospital? Would it make any difference? Would I be able to cope with being in there? I guess the only way I was going to get answers to these questions was by being brave and just going into hospital. The next day, I don't know why, I went into work. I was going to ring the ward and tell them that I would be in on Saturday, because I needed to get a few things first. When I went into work, Stella told me that someone had rung me at work the previous afternoon at 5.30pm - I thought that it must have been someone from the hospital. When I told my colleagues that there was a bed available and I intended going in on Saturday, they couldn't see why I had come into work. They thought I should go into hospital straightaway, so I left work and decided I would go into town to get all the items that I needed to take into hospital with me. All the time I was in town I kept thinking "Why am I going? I can't go in." Nevertheless, when I got home, I packed everything I needed and then sat downstairs watching TV. I thought that it would be dinner-time, and then snack- time, and then I would go in. I was just putting off going to hospital as long as I could, thinking about the meals, the food, and not exercising; "I will not last long there" I thought to myself.

I eventually told myself that I had to go, so I rang for a taxi. I arrived at the hospital at 4.45 pm. One of the nurses told me that that was very late, but she took me up to the ward where I went through the usual questions.

I was asked what I was going to order for dinner, and I made my order. I wrote in my diary on 23rd October

2008: *"Admission to hospital. After going into hospital, knowing there was a bed for me, I guess I thought everyone would say that it would be alright for me to keep working if I wasn't sure about going in. When I arrived, I saw the doctor who asked the same old questions. The girls seemed really nice, everyone had been friendly. I am feeling angry because everyone is on my case, but if I think about it, they are only doing it because they care".* The first few days were really difficult and it was hard to adjust. I knew some, but not all, of the staff. Even though I knew what the routine was it was still a struggle. The first few days I struggled with the meals, which were disgusting. I didn't know the other patients that well, because I had only just come onto the ward and it would take me a while to get to know them all.

I had a visit from Kelly and I found it really difficult; I nearly burst into tears when she left. That's one of the reasons I have to continue this treatment, because I hate getting upset; it feels uncomfortable and it seems to be more painful to cry, for blocking out all my emotions seems to be less painful. The children at work had made me a book, or rather the staff had, all working together - a small 'get well' book with messages inside. I looked at the book the first weekend I was in hospital, and I got upset when I read their messages. I will treasure the book forever.

I was given a named nurse, whom I already knew, and I found it easy to talk to her. I couldn't open up completely to her, but at least I felt comfortable enough to talk to her. I had to be weighed; I knew and understood why I had to be weighed, but I don't think that I can be assessed by what I weigh. Anyway my body mass index has got to be high; I don't know what it is, but I am certain that it is very high. I also saw the dietician who sets the meals for everyone, stage 1 is for when you first come into hospital, then you go onto stage 2. The dietician was very good to talk to because she advised me about meals. I believed what she said about meals and weight gain, but I don't think my genes are normal. I wouldn't gain any weight, especially if I stopped eating, and the fact that I am going through the menopause early meant that I was going to gain weight - that was why I am the size I am.

While I was in hospital I was going to have a test on my heart, to see if everything was alright, and also a blood test. The first week there seemed to be the longest week in my life. Every morning we had a group session where all the patients got together to discuss whether we wanted to talk about ourselves. I found the group useful on some days. There was a ward round every week which gave a chance to discuss any problems with the consultant and other professional people involved. The first week I didn't request anything, so I went into my first ward round saying and expecting nothing. I coped fairly well the first week - always the easy period for me - but it is the next few weeks when I start to struggle, because I miss going to the gym and exercising.

The second week after my admission I attended a group I had never been to before, namely a nutrition group, held every Tuesday morning. I was interested to find out what the group was about. The group talked about food labels and the fact that they never had the correct information on it i.e. the calories in the food. I always look at the calories on anything that I eat. The nutritionist said that we needed at least 2000 calories every day. There was also the use of the gym which is where I make the biggest mistake. When I go to the gym I make sure I burn off 2000 calories on the cardio machine. I use the stepping machine, running and rowing machines, the cross trainer and the bikes. I also know the 'Body Attack' class will burn off 500 calories, and the spinning classes will burn off 400 calories. The dietician also said that the equipment is not always correct because everyone has a different body type. This information was very useful, but I was not altogether sure about all the things she was telling us on this subject. The body image group was also interesting, but I was not sure how useful it was. We learnt how this illness could affect the body, and also how we saw our bodies, i.e. wearing big clothes or lots of layers. I found the group very difficult and struggled to concentrate most of the time. I don't think I got much out of it.

By the end of the second week I wanted to have some time out but I knew that it would be at least two weeks before I could have any leave. I wasn't sure whether I could last that long, but I knew I couldn't leave. I had to somehow stick it out as long as I could. I had a lot of visitors and I had a good time with them. I caught up with what was going on, and I told them about how it was going in hospital. I tried to explain it as best as I could. Kelly came to visit in the first two weeks. I never told my family about going into hospital; I was too ashamed and embarrassed to say anything to them, for they did not know anything about eating disorders, and they told me that I had got to sort myself out. I get really angry when people have this attitude, because my family know that I wasn't like this when I was younger. If I could stop it, I would, because it is not a pleasant illness. I want to get better, rather than spend the rest of my life going in and out of hospital. I feel I cannot understand or gain a real insight into this illness. That's why a lot of the time I get on with my life, and keep myself to myself. Anyway, I made contact with them and they came to visit me, although I didn't know what to say to them. I tried not to talk about the illness, as there was no point. My cousin Rachel visited and I am not sure just how much she understood, but she always supported me. Rachel tried to help me and to be there for me. She had been very supportive and close to my mum, and had always visited her; mum knew that Rachel would be there for her.

By week 3 I had become really irritable, angry with the place and with everyone there. All I ever seemed to do was eat, and it seemed like one meal after another. I was becoming more and more annoyed, because I was now missing the gym. Also I didn't want to be eating all this food without being able to exercise. I was concerned that I had to exercise to eat. There were times when I had to leave the dining-room because of something someone had said. I had to sit in the room and calm down.

The next morning I thought I was going to leave. I couldn't stay here anymore; but after one of the nurses spoke to me, I would calm down. This is how much I have changed since my previous stay in hospital, because then I would have just left. Now I think about what happens, and work out why I want to go home; there's no point doing that, so I have to stay here and get the help I need. At this stage I would see a lot of positive change in me, knowing that I had a long way to go and that I had to keep working at it. All I could do was make the most of my admission. The fact that I was gaining weight always scared me when I went into hospital. The dietician tried to reassure me, saying that it is because my body is trying to hold on to water, because I don't drink regularly or often enough during the day. I really hated the focus on weight, however.

On one morning, after a really bad night, I felt sick. I had my blood pressure checked, and found that it was really high. I was also having chest pains. A doctor came to see me, and I was sent over to the A & E department. When they checked me over and did an ECG, the results came back clear, and I returned to the ward. The experience scared me a lot, making me think about the future. I thought about what recovery would be like so I looked at the advantages and disadvantages of recovery:

Advantages	Disadvantages
1. It helps me to feel in control (exercising and eating).	1. I am often tired.
2. I feel good about the way I can control my feelings.	2. I feel weak a lot of the time.
3. I am able to control my emotions when I lost dad, George and mum.	3. Not being able to accept invites from friends for dinner.
4. People often believed and said what a strong person I was.	4. Not being able to go anywhere with friends because I feel they will force me to eat and drink.
5. I can keep my anger away.	5. Not being able to go out with friends because a fear of not going to the gym.

I looked at this diagram and I could clearly see that there were more advantages than disadvantages. If the disadvantages were gone, I would have a much better quality of life, and I would be able to stop dragging myself through every day. I felt that it was important for me to do this exercise, so that I could see for myself the advantages and disadvantages of having this illness. I wanted to have some leave this weekend because it was the end of the third week, but the doctors said I had to do a month before I could have any time away. I had taken leave early on previous occasions, and I had more time out than I should have had. Sometimes I didn't go back at all, so I had to see the month out before I would be allowed to have any time out. Time seemed to go so slowly in hospital - there were only so many 1000 piece jigsaws that I could do. I had already completed one, and was half-way through my second one. I was also missing the gym and the exercising. I was desperate to get back into my classes, instead of sitting here eating and getting fat.

I couldn't really talk to anyone about how frustrated I was getting, and how I needed to get out, just to do something, even one exercise class would help me. Part of my problem over the years was that I hadn't really opened up enough when I was in hospital. I should have tried to find one member of staff who could help me get my feelings out; it would have helped if they understood how I was feeling.

I had two ECG tests while I was in hospital; one was fine, and the other showed some irregular heart beats or something else which was not really serious. I also had a 24-hour tape to monitor my heart, to see if there was any problem. The results of this test came back all clear too, which I was happy about, because at least I could carry on with my exercising. I don't know what I would have done if I had been told I that I couldn't exercise any more.

At the beginning of week four I was able to ask for time out at the weekend, even if it was only for a few hours. Brian and Stella said that they would come and take me home for a few hours at the weekend. I was just happy to get out of there for a short time.

I had a lot of visitors whilst I was in hospital, including my managers. Kelly visited me a lot and she was very supportive. Rachel came every week too. Mark visited me a couple of times and then there was Anna, Richard and Kirsty - so I got a lot of visitors; it was nice to know that a lot of people were thinking of me, wanting to support me.

When my weekend off came I couldn't wait to get out. I knew I wouldn't be able to exercise, but at least I could get home and change some of my clothes. So Brian picked me up and brought me home, and took me back to the hospital later. When I was in hospital I had a lot of time and space to think about how the illness was affecting me. I was able to think about how I was feeling inside. I did a box to reflect how I was feeling:

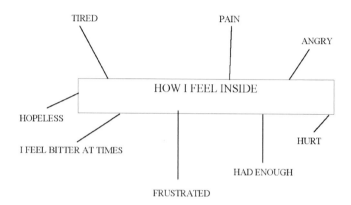

TIRED

PAIN

ANGRY

HOW I FEEL INSIDE

HOPELESS

I FEEL BITTER AT TIMES

HURT

HAD ENOUGH

FRUSTRATED

I know some of these feelings have been inside me for some time - ever since my dad died. Because it had been so long ago, I didn't want to dig these feelings out; I wasn't sure that I would ever be able to handle them. I knew that I would have to move on in my life, and by holding on to this illness, I could carry on. I knew that it was not healthy and my body would not allow me to keep doing this, but I couldn't handle the thought of letting go. Long-term health problems would not be good for me.

On week 5, I was given a discharge date. I was happy about that, but also nervous. I realised that I had changed, and the fact that I had managed to stay in hospital and be given a discharge date made me proud of myself. I know there had been many days when I was in hospital that I was ready to walk away, but I never did. I kept on reminding myself that I needed to stay in hospital, and work on my problems and stop running away from them all the time. Sometimes the doctors discussed with me about having more therapy, but I wasn't keen. I really felt I had had enough therapy, and I didn't feel I needed any more one-to-one. They wanted me to at least think about it, so I agreed to consider it.

We continued to have the nutritional group work, looking

at what each food group did for the body, such as why we need fats in our diet. One of the interesting sections was about chocolate, and why it is good for us; this surprised me. I found this group very interesting, although some of the things the dietician told us made me raise my eyebrows, but I thought "She is the expert so she must know what she is talking about." I think I have told and conditioned myself into believing food was bad. I just couldn't believe anything else.

While I was in hospital, I wished I could have been strong enough to write about some of the pain I was experiencing so that the staff could help me more. If only I wasn't so proud and strong-willed I might have been able to let some of my thoughts and feelings out. I was able to write some of them, however, on a piece of paper which I gave to one of the nurses. I had weekend leave for the first time - it was going to be a Saturday afternoon, until the Sunday afternoon. I was looking forward to being in my own environment, and I really wanted to exercise. I didn't say anything to the nurses about how I felt; I knew what they would have said anyway, and I was worried that they wouldn't let me have any leave, so I didn't let on to anyone. When Saturday afternoon came along I couldn't wait to get out; once at home I dropped all my bags off and went straight out again.

I did some shopping at my local shopping centre since it was getting near to Christmas; all the shops were busy. There were Christmas lights and everything looked pretty and bright. I don't know why, but I thought everything looked beautiful and it made me realise that I didn't want to be in and out of hospital, cut off from the outside world. I spent the rest of Saturday night just chilling out at home and watching the television. I didn't follow the eating plan; I just had a snack before I went to bed. I didn't go to the gym either, which was a positive step for me. I knew that it was going to take time and that I would only take one step at a time. I had a text from Stella who wanted to know if she and Tina could come round and visit. Tina was the coordinator of the Baby Unit; she was leaving to go to live in Germany and wanted to visit me before she left. I said that it would be fine to visit and to come at 2pm, I needed to go to the gym and to my class first.

On Sunday morning I left for the 'body attack' class, and felt great about being back. I spoke to some of the girls in the class; they asked me where I had been. I said I hadn't been very well and left it at that. I enjoyed the class and then went over to the gym. I did a few hours' exercise and then I rushed to the shops to get something for Stella and Tina to have when they visited. When I got home, I thought about whether I wanted to go back to the hospital. I felt I did not fit in, seeing myself as having a normal body shape and size. When I am in hospital, I think that I am obese. I feel so uncomfortable about my size and I feel so greedy. I feel fat for eating all the food. I was at home now and was able to eat as much as I felt comfortable with; I felt safe doing that. At 2.00pm Stella and Tina arrived; it was nice to see them, and we chatted and had a laugh. We talked about my eating problem and I explained it was still a bit of a struggle, but I was working on it. I tried to keep it really short because they didn't really understand and I didn't want to talk about it. We had a good time, listened to some CDs, had a laugh, and then Stella said she would take me back. Although I agreed, I didn't really want her to drive me back as I could make my own way on the bus. I think that she felt I wouldn't go back. When we arrived at the hospital, they stayed with me for a short time and then left. I went back on the ward and chatted to the other girls about my weekend. I didn't mention that I had been exercising and how much I had eaten.

I just felt everything was fine: the girls on the ward were really nice, and I could talk to them; there were times when we laughed and joked together, which was important in that environment. We were also there for each other; we all had bad days and we would support each other through those times. I found it interesting that one of the girls who had an eating disorder had a career helping people and supporting others. I found that interesting, because we all seem to struggle to cure ourselves or else we beat ourselves up - as I have done for most of my life.

The next day when we had our morning group session we were asked about our leave and how it had gone. I didn't say much, just that it went alright but I had struggled with some of the meals. I felt like a total fraud. I guess that since I've had an eating disorder for so long, I have learnt not to be honest about everything, though I know that is not always the best way and it was not going to help me. I thought that if I had said how everything had really gone, I would feel like a failure in the group. I had a one-to-one session with one of the nurses, which is something all the girls have, but I didn't open up fully; I said that I struggled over the weekends because I find it difficult buying meals. I do find it hard to choose meals, even though the nurses gave me ideas. I thought that I was not doing myself any good by opening up, for I was worried about how I would be viewed. I felt I would fall apart if I let go of this illness. It was this thought that was now holding me together.

When I saw my consultant that week we talked about future therapy. I was still very unsure about it; but he still wanted me to think about it, saying that therapy didn't work overnight and could take several years to be effective. I agreed to keep thinking about it. He then asked me how I was coping on the ward, and I said it was still a struggle at meal times and that I found it really hard. He said that it would take a long time, because I had had the illness for such a long time. I also talked about my exercising and how I was struggling with it, because I didn't want to be seen as a failure. I always found it easy and comfortable to speak to my consultant for he made me feel calm. I didn't always tell him about my thoughts and feelings, however, for I found it hard to open up to people in general.

When we had a ward round that week, I asked for a long weekend at home from Friday afternoon to Sunday afternoon, and this was agreed. I was going to plan more activities for myself and maybe meet up with a few friends. I had had a hard week on the ward, for I was really finding the meals and drinks hard. There was a choice between orange juice or blackcurrant, tea or coffee, and I don't like any of them - but it was either that or nothing. I had to drink every last drop, or else start from the beginning again. I got really annoyed by this, because in the real world nobody has to make such choices - so I became frustrated and annoyed. I have always found fluids a real struggle, and that is a big problem because I can go through the day without anything to drink until I have been to the gym. After going to the gym I usually feel thirsty. One of the sessions with the dietician was about fluids and hydration shifts, which helped me to understand why my weight goes up and down. When I am in hospital my weight is everywhere, it tends to go up mostly, because I don't drink as much as I should when I am in hospital. I am drinking more in the day than I usually do, so my body holds on to the fluid. The dietician said that weight gain is the body holding on to the fluids - that is what she explained. We also learnt how dangerous dehydration is. I found all this information useful, though I sometimes tell myself that I don't need to know all this because hearing about the dangers and what can happen, means I will have to face it and deal with it. I can't just ignore it, which is what I want to do.

We also had an activity group. On one occasion we made plans to go out of the hospital and visit the German market in the city centre which is held before Christmas. I was looking forward to this visit. Four of us went to the German Market; we were all rather quiet on the way there, perhaps because we all thought one of the nurses would be with us throughout the trip. I think we were also thinking about the leave that we all had at the weekend.

When we arrived in the town it was dark and it was also raining, so it wasn't a good evening, but I wanted to make the best of it. I was surprised when the nurses said "Right, girls, we will meet back here at 3.00 p.m." I thought they were going to follow us around for the whole 30 minutes. When the nurses left, we all smiled at each other and made our way down to the market. I enjoyed looking at the jewellery, which was beautiful. We all stuck together as a group and looked at each stall together. When we had finished exploring the market, I said I would pop into a local CD store. The rest of the girls said they would come with me, so we all went together. I bought a CD, and two of the other girls bought something too. Then we all made our way back to meet the nurses. I enjoyed our trip out, but I was not really sure of the point of it in terms of treatment and therapy; but I had enjoyed it, and it gave us the chance to get to know each other even better.

On Friday I couldn't wait till 3.15 pm when I would be able to leave hospital for the weekend. The morning seemed to last forever - sitting time went on for 2 hours instead of one. Eventually I had a snack and was able to leave. By the time I got home it was 5.30 pm, so I chilled out in front of the television. It was so nice to watch what I wanted to watch. I had a snack in front of the television in my living room, feeling relaxed rather than stressed in the hospital dining room. I was really looking forward to the weekend at home.

On Saturday morning I woke up quite early, eager to get to my 'Body Attack' class and then the gym. I had a good workout, and then came home and rang some friends just to catch up. In the afternoon I met a friend and we went to the cinema; I enjoyed the film. When I leave the hospital I tend to go back to the things I shouldn't be doing. I really struggle with the illness on my own. I don't know if it is because I can get away with it in the normal world, because I don't look as if I have a problem. I am quite big, so nobody can tell that I have an eating disorder. After I came home from the cinema all I had was a sandwich and a few drinks. I don't seem to be able to take control of this illness - it just rules me.

When I come out of hospital I go back to my usual environment and maybe that has a lot to do with it. The memories are all around me, and because I have never come to terms with my losses, I cannot change, or it is very difficult to do so. I know that I will need a lot of support which I find really hard because I find it really hard to trust anyone. With an eating disorder, friends and family tend to walk away or say something stupid and dumb like, "You just have to eat". I have been talking to the girls on the ward, and they all say the same thing, that friends and family lose patience and tell you to sort yourself out. This really upsets me. I know I have to do this and nobody can do it for me, but I can't actually do it on my own. I am going to need everyone's support - friends and family - to help me through this difficult time.

I appreciate it when someone sees me take a bit of something to eat or drink says "Well done". This helps me to try again. If I saw someone who had broken their leg, and they had just had the cast removed, and they were able to take a few steps, I would say "Well done, you are doing well". I would continue to praise them and support them for months, because I know it would take a long time for them to regain their confidence to be on their feet again. I sometimes feel that because I have an eating disorder and I have a lot of treatment, I am expected to be fully recovered from this condition and over it by now. I am frustrated with all this now. I want my life back, but I am finding it a really big struggle. I am not going to give up, however, because I know if I do, I'll have a lot of medical problems.

On Sunday morning I got up and did my usual routine of

'Body Attack' and then the gym for two hours. I was in the gym when I thought about the week ahead in hospital. I thought about whether I could go back to hospital. I was feeling like this because I had had a really good weekend. I had managed to catch up with friends; I had been to the cinema, and had a good time. Although I had done 6 hours in the gym and with my classes there, it was something I enjoyed doing. I know that I do not perform my exercise in the correct way, for I use it to burn fat (which I have a lot of) and to block my emotions out of my head, because I can't get rid of them any other way. After I had finished, I went home and just chilled. I tidied around the house and did some washing and spent the rest of the afternoon watching some football on the TV.

I got my clothes sorted out ready to take back to hospital. At 4.30 pm I made my way back to hospital; it is never easy going back after being away for a few days, because when I go back I go into a pretend world. I just tell them some of what they want to hear, not everything. I went to my room, and then I went to the lounge area and sat with some of the girls. I caught up with them and how their weekends went. Everyone seemed to have had a good time. I said to myself that even if they had really struggled, they wouldn't have said anything to me, because that is how we are. In a way we all try to be perfect in every way - we cannot admit we have a problem, or that we have failed. I hate it, feeling really stupid when I do something wrong, or when I fail at doing something and someone corrects me.

After tea, one of the nurses came to me to have a bit of a chat about my weekend. I said that it was a struggle, and she asked me what I'd had to eat that day. I said that I had had a salad bowl, a snack and a drink. The nurse said to me that it was not enough. While I was sitting there trying to listen to what she was saying to me, I thought to myself, "There is no way that I can eat at home the way I eat when I am in hospital";

Example of one day's hospital menu for me:

Meals
Breakfast (8:15am)
4 slices of toast (brown bread) with butter
Bowl of Weetabix, Cornflakes or Shredded Wheat with a glass of orange juice and cup of coffee

Snack Time
10:15am – cup of tea

Lunch Time (could be 12:30)
Quiche, vegetables, potatoes with a drink

Snack Time
(around 3:15) cup of tea

Dinner (around 5:30pm)
Macaroni cheese, potatoes, sweetcorn with a drink

Snack (7:30pm)
Two digestive biscuits, with a drink

This is a typical meal that I would have in hospital. Some days I really struggled, because I restricted myself so much, and I didn't eat the amount they expected me to in hospital. I struggled a lot with fluids, the orange and blackcurrant was always really watered down and it tasted disgusting. The coffee and tea didn't taste any better. My biggest fear was gaining a lot of weight in hospital. My weight was around 10½ stones – I never knew for sure because I always refused to be told. I was scared to eat that amount during the day because it was not normal, and no-one ate in that way. All I could do was to try my best – every mouthful was a battle and I had to keep saying to myself, "I need to get well; I am not coming back to this place again".

The nurse continued to talk to me about the changes I had to make to be able to keep myself well. I felt a bit flat after we had our meetings. I didn't mention all the exercise that I did at the weekend - I didn't think it was worth it, and I couldn't explain how I felt and what drove me to exercise so much. I had just over a week left in hospital now, and all I could do was make the most of it and try to get as much as possible from the stay. When I saw the dietician she agreed to me being weighed just once a week. "I don't know why I need to be weighed, anyway" I said to her; but I agreed to it. Metabolic rate refers to the rate at which a person uses energy. I found this section very interesting - a person who is heavier has a much higher metabolic rate because muscle uses more energy than fat. Also the less food that anyone eats, the more likely they will be to stop losing weight. What I understood from this section was that the body protects itself to help it survive with less food i.e. it tries to get as much energy and calories as possible. This was hard for me to understand; I think I am really afraid and it worries me when I go to hospital; I always seem to gain a lot of weight, but I now know that it can happen like that over a short time. It is very hard to take all of this in, however. I decided to take the handouts away with me, and read the information again for myself. We also had a body image group where they discussed the Minnesota study and its relevance to eating disorders.

This refers to an experiment that was done in 1950 in which they starved a group of men who were healthy and had no mental health problems. These men volunteered to take part in this experiment; they ate normally for the first three months while their eating patterns, their personalities and their moods were examined. During the next 6 months the men were restricted to half of their normal food intake. They lost 25% of their body weight. The next 3 months the men were re-nourished. It was found from the experiment that there was a notable change in their social, physical and psychological behaviour due to starvation. The men no longer could tell that they were hungry, and this led them to binge on food. I now understood that when I restrict my intake I become very confused, moody and even angry. I related to a lot of this because I find it hard to concentrate, and I know that at times I am very irritable. I become very withdrawn, and I isolate myself a lot in order to cope with everything. The physical changes that I notice in myself are lack of sleep and occasional headaches, and this is all because of my eating disorder - I am unable to think straight, and if I am not eating, I am still exercising a lot. I cannot function well enough to sort out any emotional problems that I have. I thought again that this session was very good, with a lot for me to think about when I left. I again took handouts to read later. I saw one of the nurses who was an Occupational Therapist, with whom I could discuss any problems that I had; she also helped me plan a light lunch on the ward, ready for my return to work.

I wasn't sure what to expect from the session, and I was a bit nervous about it, though the Occupational Therapist made me feel really relaxed. We went to another section of the hospital, where there was a room with a cooker, a dining room table, and cupboards. I had to butter two slices of bread; when I put the butter on, she told me to put more on. I didn't know why they had to make such a big issue about the butter and how much we should use - another one of their annoying traits! I then put the tuna on the bread, and I cut the bread into halves to make a sandwich. I poured myself a drink of apple juice - something different (wow!). After I prepared my lunch, the nurse prepared hers, and we sat together to eat. While we ate, we chatted about what we enjoyed watching on television; it was all very relaxing, and wasn't as difficult as I thought it would be. We had a chat later that day about how I had felt about that activity, and I said that I had found it easy to do, except that I had had a bit of an issue about the amount of butter I needed to put on my bread. I never have liked having a lot of butter on my bread. I would rather have none at all, but I don't think that is to do with my eating disorder, more with the problem I have eating lunch at work, because maybe my body has got used to me not having regular food during the day. The main thing that I said to the nurse was that I really wanted to change the way I did things at work, because I was fed up with the amount of time I was having off with the illness.

I decided to go back to work and really give it a go. One of the head psychiatrists came to talk to me; he had seen me before in Out-Patients and wanted to find out why I didn't want to have any more therapy. I felt I had gone as far as I could with that side of my treatment, but he thought that I hadn't yet sorted out my issues. He talked to me about my dad, George and my mum and I told him how I felt about their deaths; he felt I still hadn't really grieved for any of them. He said I needed more therapy to come to terms with these things, and that unless I dealt with all the emotional issues that were keeping me in this eating disorder, I would never get over it and move on with my life. I agreed with what he had to say to me, but I didn't really want to go into more therapy. I always find it hard, and at times it is really painful.

I said that I would have a think about it, and I would let him know what I had decided in the morning. At the end of the day after 9.30 pm snacks I did my "sitting time" which was half-an-hour later ("sitting time" is to encourage us not to exercise to use up the calories that have just been taken in - this is done for one hour after a main meal). I was tired and I was thinking about what to do about future therapy. I went to my room, had a shower and got ready to go to bed. That night I thought about the benefits of more therapy, even though I didn't find it that easy to open up to anyone. I just didn't fancy the idea of going into therapy again, and decided that I wouldn't have any more treatment. I managed to get some rest that night.

The following morning after breakfast one of the nurses said she would catch up with me, for she wanted to see how I was doing. The nurse started to talk about my weight, and how it was increasing. At that point I was getting more and more angry. I thought, "What the hell are you are trying to say - that I was making this illness up? Yes, I know that I am gaining weight and I am fat, you don't have to tell me that". I think a lot of these professional people see someone with an eating disorder and they think of a 5 stone person with this problem, but I don't see it like that. She wanted to talk about other issues also. What I wanted to say in the ward round was that she should get out of my face and leave. I was quite upset after she left, but I thought that I was going home soon, so it was not worth getting upset about it; but I was really annoyed. I kept myself to myself, and I tried to focus on my three thousand piece jigsaw puzzle. I know that this sometimes stops me from climbing up the wall in this place. I managed to catch up with the head psychiatrist; I told him that I didn't feel that I needed to have more therapy. He said that I would find more treatment helpful, especially if I talked about my dad's death (which I am still finding very hard to do) and the two other bereavements, but I just did not want to talk about them anymore.

I just felt it was time to move on with my life and forget about the bereavements. I don't think he was very impressed with what I had said, but I had to be honest with him. There was no point in saying I would have more therapy when I didn't want to. After our meeting, I went back on the ward and saw one of the girls in the lounge. I asked her if she wanted to chat. Holly was a young girl - I am not sure how old she was, probably in her mid-twenties. She was about 5'5 tall inches tall and quite attractive. I asked her how long she had had this illness, and she said she couldn't remember not having it. She had been in day care for a long time, but it hadn't helped her, and she had been an out-patient for a long time. I told her I had been in hospital 3 times before, and I said that I also had had this problem a long time and had been in hospital a few times, but that this was my best stay because I had stuck to it and not walked away. Holly said she wanted to sort it out because she did not want to come into hospital again. I said that was the right thing to do with this illness. It was really good to talk to her; one of the good things in hospital was that other girls on the ward were nice and friendly. We all supported each other, and all the girls are really easy to approach. It was great to sit up and watch DVDs together in the evening, and just be able to relax at the end of the day, after all the meals and the therapy, the groups, the dieticians and doctors.

I had to start to think about how I was going to start eating at work; I wasn't looking forward to it, because I find it very hard to eat with people I know around me. I really feel nervous, thinking they are watching me eat and looking at what I eat, but I wanted to try hard this time. I managed to have a chat to the Occupational Therapist about my return to work; she was quite positive about it, telling me to take one day at a time and not to set myself high goals. I wanted to be positive about it, and I wasn't going to worry too much; yet I had to wait until I was discharged from hospital. I still had a bit of work to do here. When I had my meeting with the consultant this week, we talked about my discharge date from hospital, which was only a week away. When he talked about my exercising, I was honest and said that I thought it was still going to be a problem for me. He said I should try to do 5 minutes less every time I went to the gym, and I agreed - "If only it was that easy", I thought to myself. We also talked about my return to work. I said that I was nervous about it, although I really wanted to go back, and was looking forward to it. He reassured me about it, and we talked about things that would help me, like a place where I could go to eat, and times also – he was always very helpful. During the final week the nutritional group looked at general nutrition, food groups, and what their functions are. There are 6 basic nutrients which are all essential for optimal health. They are minerals, proteins, carbohydrates, vitamins and fats. If I limit my intake and only eat some of these foods, I will not meet my nutritional needs. We were told about how each of these nutritional groups help, and what happens when one does not take in enough of these 6 basic nutrients – the body won't work properly.

I found this group very interesting and useful, for the dietician who led the group was really good and helpful. The "body image" group also finished this week. We went over the subjects that we had been taught, and also talked about what we wanted to do the following week. We had a choice of the German Market in town, which some of us had already visited, or to go bowling. Most of the group wanted to go bowling. I was not sure about the "body image" group, for I didn't learn or get much from it, nor did I find it as interesting. I was told about a support group that was being held every Wednesday evening for day care patients and for patients who had been discharged. On Wednesday evening I was allowed to attend, together with one of the other girls. We had both got our discharge date. There were only three of us in the group with two members of staff also. I talked a little about myself, describing my exercise addiction, and they all offered me advice which I could try. The group lasted for one hour. It was very similar to the one I used to attend before at the hospital.

This time the group had been set up for patients who had just left the hospital or had left day care. When we got back to the ward I was speaking to one of the girls from the ward, who had attended the group. She asked me why I didn't talk to the physiotherapist about my exercise; I said to her "Can they help? What will they offer me?" She said she had had a problem with exercise and they had given her an exercise programme to follow. She said she had struggled with it, but the programme had helped her. I thought it was worth talking to the physiotherapist about my exercise programme to see what they would come up with.

At ward round this week I said that I wanted to go home from Friday afternoon to Monday night, because I wanted to go into work to see everyone. I was really nervous about going back to work. My biggest worry was the eating. How was I going to develop an eating plan at work? How was I going to maintain it? Could I eat with anyone at work without feeling uncomfortable? Would I be able to trust them enough to think that were not watching me? I would just have to wait and see how things went. I made my request for my weekend leave, and they said it was alright, so I was really looking forward to it. The Occupational

Therapist went over my plans for the weekend. I said I could try a meal with chicken, sweetcorn and peas for one meal, tuna pasta for another, and for breakfast, cornflakes. I thought to myself at least I was going to try; but there was no way I was going to eat as much food as I did in hospital. I knew I had a lot of hard work to do with my eating disorder.

I was hoping to have a chat with one of the physiotherapists when I went back to the ward after my weekend leave. I left the ward at 3.30 pm on Friday for my weekend leave, went straight home and had a nice relaxing evening in. On Saturday I got up as usual, and thought about having some breakfast, but then I thought I would have something when I got back. I did my usual exercise class, then I did 2 hours in the gym. Afterwards I went into the city centre to do some Christmas shopping. It was very busy and the shops were crowded as you would expect at that time of the year. I then went to my local supermarket and bought a few items like sandwiches, chicken, and something to drink.

When I got home I had a sandwich to eat with a drink and some snacks. During the evening I had one or two drinks and some snacks. I realised that I should be eating more than I had eaten, but I had at least eaten better than previously. On Sunday I attended an hour class and the gym for two hours, then met a few people whom I hadn't seen for a long time. I had a chat with them in between the class and the gym. That is the thing about going to the gym - I meet different people and have a chat and a laugh with them, so I am not as isolated as everyone seems to make me out to be. I spent the rest of the day at home; I watched a DVD, and had some chicken and a drink for my lunch. In the evening I had a drink and a tin of pears which I had in the cupboard. I had a snack before I went to bed. This may not have been as much as I should have eaten, but it was better than nothing.

On the Monday I woke a bit earlier than usual, because I wanted to do some tidying around the house. When I finished I left for the gym, and did the usual cardio exercises on the cross-trainer, treadmill, rower and stepper. When I left, I went back to work to see everyone. It was really strange being back at work. The children seemed to have grown a lot since I went away. I spent a few hours at work with the staff and children just to give myself a look in at work again. When I left work, I went to my

'Body Attack' class, and then went home. I'd had a bad day because I hadn't stuck to any eating plan. When I got home I only had a bowl of soup. I popped out to see one of my neighbours who had been keeping an eye on the house for me, and spent an hour and a half with her, talking about how my treatment was going. I didn't really want to go back to hospital. I had got used to not having these rules about how much you have to drink and having to complete meals and feeling so controlled in the dining room, where I felt so uncomfortable anyway. My neighbour said I had done really well. This coming week I would be discharged, so it was only going to be a few more days on the ward. I had a friend who said she would take me back to the hospital, and she took me at 8.30 pm. When I arrived I went to say hello to the girls, but by the time I had told them how my time out had gone it was time for a snack. I had a snack, watched a bit of TV in the lounge, then went to my room to get ready for bed.

Although I didn't feel tired I had a shower and I did some reading. I also thought about the future.

I had to think about how I was going to deal with work.

I had to look at what recovery is or will be:

1. Being able to find freedom from the fear of food.
2. Being able to go out with friends and socialise without being afraid of food or drink.
3. Being able to visit friends without being worried about being offered a drink.
4. Not feeling greedy for having food or drinks if I am offered them.
5. Not feeling guilty, fat and lazy because I missed the gym.
6. Being able to feel confident in my body and with myself.
7. Being able to plan the future and look forward to the future.
8. Being able to stop feeling trapped.
9. Being able to deal with my feelings in a healthier way not connected with food.
10. Being able to deal with anger in a positive way.
11. Have fun in life.
12. Being able to deal with the loss of people I have loved and to hold onto all the good times, knowing that my family would

always live on in my heart.

13. Being able to accept the things that I cannot change.

14. Being able to accept that I am not perfect and when I make mistakes that it is alright.

It was also important to look at what recovery is not:

1. Recovery is not an instant fix, but accepting that it won't happen overnight.

2. Realising that since I live on my own it's going to be hard dealing with my emotions and eating properly, knowing that if I have a bad day I have to try not to let it affect my eating (that will be easier said than done).

3. Trying not to think about the past all the time because that will not help me.

4. Not being afraid of food

5. Not being angry with myself all the time

6. Not hating myself and trying to take out everything that goes wrong on my body.

7. Restricting food.

8. Exercising too much.

By the time I finished doing this it was midnight, but it was important for me to look at what I hoped to get out of all this, and the one big thing for me was that I had stayed in the hospital and followed the programme. Yes, I have had days when I could have quite easily walked out. I have gone into my room and cried. I have got angry in that dining-room and not completed my meal, but I didn't walk out of the place. I have now realised that I have this illness which I need to deal with - if I don't, I will end up really ill or something more serious will happen. There was no point in me walking out and going home; that was not going to help me, so I stayed, and here I am after nearly 7 weeks in hospital. I thought that whatever happens, when I go home I can look back on this hospital stay and be pleased with myself, knowing that I have done it, and it has made me stronger. It has helped me to realise why I have this illness and what functions it has in my life.

Functions of my eating disorder in my life

1. It allows me to stay in control of my life.
2. It allows me to keep my anger under control.
3. It helps me function every day, restricting my eating and over-exercising.
4. It has become my best friend; it never lets me down.
5. It blocks out my emotions and thoughts.

The following day I had to try and catch one of the physiotherapists, so I spent the morning looking out for them. Whilst I was waiting, one of the Occupational Therapists came to see me to have a chat about how my weekend leave had gone. I told her how my leave had gone; she was not impressed with my eating plans, saying that I would have to eat more than that when I went back to work. I knew this, but I would have to take one day at a time if I'm to recover from this illness, which I know is going to be really hard. I managed to catch one of the physiotherapists when she came onto the ward, and I asked her if I could have a chat regarding my exercise programme; she said she would come up to the ward later. That just made me nervous about seeing her. Most of us were looking forward to our trip, for it was the 'body image' evening. I wasn't sure whether I was looking forward to the evening - it was the thought of the nursing staff being around. Would they be watching us all night? After dinner the physiotherapist was able to see me. I explained to her about my exercising, and asked if there was anything that she could suggest. She asked me when I was going home; when I said "tomorrow", she said it did not give her enough time to plan a programme, but she was sure that I needed some sort of programme to follow. She said to leave it with her and she would work out some sort of programme for me, and would get back to me tomorrow.

After I saw the physiotherapist I thought about my current exercise routine, which usually had two different activities:

SUNDAY	MONDAY	TUESDAY	WEDNESDAY
1 hour Body Attack 1 hour Gym	1 hour Body Attack 1 hour Bums and Tums	1½ hours Gym 1 hour Studio Cycling	1½ hours Gym 1 hour Body Attack
THURSDAY	**FRIDAY**	**SATURDAY**	Total: 16 hours weekly
1 ½ hours Gym 1 hour Studio Cycling	2 hours Gym	2 hours Gym 1 hour Studio Cycling	

I asked myself whether I would cut it down and do less? I began to worry about it a lot because I knew I wouldn't be able to allow myself to eat and drink because of the fear of gaining a lot of weight and feeling fat and greedy. It was at this point that I realised I had a lot of mental work to do, and still had a long way to go.

I just have to see how it goes when I am discharged. On the ward all the girls were looking forward to our night out bowling. We went in two taxis and all played together in one alley. The evening wasn't as bad as I thought it was going to be; I thought the staff would be watching us, but they weren't - they joined in and played with us. We played one game, then had to make our way back to the hospital. It took a while for the taxis to arrive. Whilst we were waiting for the taxis to arrive, I had the chance to have a chat with one of the girls. I asked her what she wanted to do when she left hospital; she said she wasn't sure, because she had been in and out of hospital for the last 5 years. When I asked her whether she thought she was better now, she said she didn't think the treatment had worked and I thought that was very sad. I sometimes wish that this illness was a lot easier, it is really hard. It is also hard for me to see others struggling with this illness.

The taxis eventually arrived, and we made our way back to the hospital. When we got back we had our evening snack, and after that I watched a bit of television then went to my room. I was happy that this was going to be my last night, and that I would be leaving tomorrow. I thought I would never be coming back to this place, but you can never tell with this illness.

The next day I woke up and packed my clothes. I had to wait until the ward round before I could leave, and that would be sometime in the morning before or after lunch. I was hoping it would be before 5 pm. After breakfast one of the physiotherapists came to see me with the programme she had worked out. I had one 'Body Attack' class, one hour in the gym and two body balance classes. I looked at it, and wondered how I could come down from what I did to this programme. I became really frustrated with this programme, because they thought changing it was really easy. I go to the gym or do classes to maintain my weight because I need to - I am too fat and it helps me cope. If I don't go to the gym, I come home from work and just sit at home gaining a lot of weight - the thought really scares me.

I would get really down. I know people say that we need hobbies, or to go to college or socialise - which I do when I go to the gym. Anyway why should I give up something that I enjoy so much? I felt a bit annoyed when the physiotherapist left the room, knowing that I would have to be coaxed to do the sort of exercise that she thought I should do. I then met with my named nurse who went over my meal plans. She said that I would have to try and eat full meals, because if I go home and continue to have salad bowls as a meal, that will lead me back to hospital. I'd have to try and eat full meals, and also eat during the day at work. I explained to her that I was going to get a lot of support at work, and she encouraged me to try really hard too. This advice I didn't listen to at the time, and I wish I had.

I called in to see the doctors at 11.00 a.m. We talked about therapy, which I had thought about a bit more; I had decided to give it another go, but my consultant said I was on the waiting list for more therapy. I thought they had already made up their minds about that. My consultant asked me when I was planning to return to work. I said that I was going back next day, and he asked me if I was sure. I said it was better for me to return to work straightaway, rather than go home and just sit around.

Anyway the sick note only covered me in the hospital, so I had to go back to work.

I asked when I could leave, and he said as soon as I got everything together. I went back on the ward and I got all my bags together. I went to see all the girls to say goodbye. I hate goodbyes. They were lovely girls and I got on with them all. I am going to miss them all.

I arrived back at home at 12.40 p.m, unpacked my bags, did some washing and sorted out all my clothes. I have to do this on my own again, but one thing I realised was that I'd have to get support from other people. I find this very difficult because I find it very hard to let anyone in to help, which isn't helping me with this illness. I just worry about my friends and family's reaction to it all, whether they will just get angry and tell me to sort it out. I already get the usual comment that only I can sort it out, which I think I know by now! I think that this is the usual reaction to me or to anyone who has this sort of problem. I am going to try my best to sort myself out, for I don't want to put any pressure on anyone.

I spent the rest of the day quietly at home. I intended to go back to the hospital to the support group, but I thought that I had better stay in and get my clothes ready for work in the morning. I popped out to get something for my evening meal, buying a quiche. I ate the quiche with a drink, which was hard for me to do. My head just told me that I'd have to try to cut back because of the weight I'd put on during my time at hospital. I should not be eating all this food - this thought went through my head every time that I put something in my mouth.

I am just going to get fatter and fatter. When these thoughts are going round in my head I can get really angry and end up saying "Stop it". It is so hard, and every time I put something in my mouth, I really have to distract myself and just go out of the house to stop myself having all these thoughts.

66. Back to Work

I didn't have much sleep that night. I was about how well I would cope back at work. How would I cope with eating at work? Would anyone say anything to upset me (about food)? I guess I was not going to have the answers to any of these questions until I went back to work.

I woke up at 7.00 a.m., ready to be at work for 8.00 a.m. I didn't have time for breakfast, but I took some sandwiches and a drink, which was a positive start for me. I wrote in my diary on day one:

"I was really very nervous. I think it was more about eating at work. I was worried about how the children would react to me, but the children were fine with me. One of the staff said something to me and I ended up snapping at her, and she went on to inform management about it. I wish they would approach me about things - they all make out that I am not approachable, and that really hurts me for I am not that sort of person. I had to have a 'Return to Work' interview, and we discussed plans for eating".

67. My Battle With Eating at Work

At my 'Return to Work' interview we talked about how they could help me. The plan was for me to meet with one of my managers and sit with her to have my lunch. I found this very difficult. It felt like they were taking over. I wanted their help and support, because I really enjoy my job, and I get a lot of job satisfaction, but I didn't know how they could help me. I just went along with the plans that they set, even though I knew it was going to be very difficult for me.

The first day didn't go well, which left me very worried about the next stage. The day was Friday, the last day of the week. When I went into work I tried to do the best I could, but I didn't feel comfortable, not really part of the team. I felt like an outsider because of the 9 weeks I'd had off during my time in hospital. I didn't know how to get involved with the rest of the team. I also felt there were big expectations on me. Everyone wanted to see me well, and eating three meals a day. I wanted to eat during the day, that was my goal, and if I could do that it would be good enough for me. I knew I wasn't going to be totally cured, and I knew that they got really angry with me. This then upset me and made me really annoyed. I couldn't follow the eating plans I made with my manager, which I know really got on her nerves. I had agreed to meet her for lunch; I didn't turn up, and she had to go and find me. I wanted help, but not in that way. A big part of me couldn't let go of this illness, because it was all that I knew. I couldn't survive without it, as my thoughts told me. I guess I believed what my mind told me, so there was always going to be a battle.

In a way it wasn't just a battle between me and management but me, management and my thoughts. I became really angry, because they thought it was easy; because I'd been in hospital, they all thought I was cured and that I should be able to get on with it. By the end of the day I wished I hadn't gone straight back. I just felt so drained. I thought it was not going to work, and was very upset when I returned home.

The whole weekend was awful - all I could think about was work, and how the first two days after returning from hospital had gone badly, though I had been really looking forward to going back. I spent most of the weekend at my fitness classes and the gym. This blocked out some of my feelings. I also began to think about why things were going wrong. As soon as I get home I go back to the same routine. I think a lot of my emotions are here in this house. There are a lot of memories here, but I know that I would find it very hard to move out, because as long as I stay here I can hold on to my mum, dad and George. I don't want to let go of them.

My eating hasn't been very good since I left hospital. I have to think that I have another chance to start again tomorrow. I am not looking forward to work, but I am going to try again to see how it goes. I didn't have much sleep again that night. I don't know why I get myself into such a state about everything - I need to take one day at a time, and to stop punishing myself when things are not going right.

I went into work on Monday morning very worried about how I was going to cope. I was still a bit annoyed with everyone, so I ended up snapping every time someone said something. When they talked about my eating, that made me even angrier.

By now I had a lot of annual leave to take, at least three weeks. I was going to ring my manager and say that I was going to take it now, and return to work after Christmas. I wasn't happy about going back to work - maybe I had gone back too soon. I rang the manager to talk to her about the way I felt about everything; she said I needed to give it a go for a bit longer and that I needed to try my best with the eating. I could see what she meant; maybe I wasn't trying hard enough with the eating. She also said that because I wasn't eating regularly this was having a big impact on my mood swings. This had also been explained to me and other patients at the hospital. This is often one of the symptoms of someone with an eating disorder, as shown by the Minnesota study of 1950. It showed that men who had quite tolerant dispositions prior to starvation gave way to frequent outbursts of anger and irritability after being starved. I didn't think I was affected like that, but I had noticed that I'd become a different person, without displaying all the signs and symptoms of this illness. Maybe I thought that I would have to be only 5 stones to be truly suffering from an eating disorder,

After talking to my manager, I just had to keep going

without trying to run away from the problem. My manager said she would be quite happy for me to eat with her in her office. I thought that was a good idea, and was grateful to her. She also suggested that I come in to work early in the morning to have something to eat before work. I saw this as a positive step forward both for me and for the staff I was working with.

On the first step of this new plan I wasn't sure what to expect. I prepared myself a cup of coffee and I brought it into the office. My manager encouraged me to have some toast with my coffee. I didn't feel very comfortable, however, and there were always the thoughts that I was fat and shouldn't be eating. I was, however, able to go down into the nursery, and I felt a lot better. I wasn't as angry now, snapping at everyone. I also had lunch with my manager in the office. I managed to eat a small amount, because I wasn't used to eating and drinking during the day. This was a real battle for me, for my thoughts were so negative - because I was eating it felt that I wasn't doing the right thing, but I did notice that it made a big difference to my moods.

I couldn't wait to get out of work at the end of the day, because I needed to get straight down to the gym to work off everything I had eaten during the day. I couldn't stand the thought that I had eaten so much, and felt disappointed with myself, thinking that I had failed. We continued to work on this plan for the next few days. I got used to it, but I never liked it much, because of the way I felt about my body and all the thoughts I had about greed, and that I shouldn't be eating all this food.

I've always felt disappointed with myself for allowing myself to eat so much food. My manager was really supportive, however, and tried to understand the illness, although sometimes I felt she was trying too hard to work out why I was the way I was. I guess I had never come to terms with the things that had happened, and I know that I have been, and still am, punishing myself for being a failure. I think that unless I am able to let go of some of these emotions, I will never be able to move on. This is difficult for me to sort out, never mind someone who doesn't know anything about the illness. Although I had just come out of hospital, I didn't talk about my emotional problems with anyone there either.

I was, however, in a much better mood to deal with the staff and much better in myself too. I found it difficult to be positive with myself when I had eaten. I was exercising as much as I could, and for as long as I could. Some days I didn't want to have lunch; some days it was a battle for me to eat in the office because I just didn't want to. I wanted to hold on to my friend (the eating disorder) as long as I could. At times I was really angry and cross with my manager; I wasn't getting cross with her because she was upsetting me, but because she was trying to take something away that had helped me cope with everything for the last 15 years of my life. How was I going to survive without it? I knew that I had to let go of it all. At the end of the day all my manager wanted to do was to help me get well, and I think that I really made good progress leading up to the Christmas break. I spent two weeks back at work on the new plan; it was very hard, but I was prepared to come back in the New Year and keep trying.

I wasn't looking forward to the Christmas break, but was determined to make the most of it. I thought about getting myself something to do, so I bought myself a 1000 piece jigsaw puzzle. I had to keep busy over the holiday. My brother Mark came to see me on Christmas Eve which was nice, and I helped him wrap up his presents. He left early on Christmas morning. Over the Christmas holiday I spent some time visiting friends. I also managed to complete my 1000 piece puzzle (that was the highlight of the holiday) even though I didn't enjoy it anymore. As soon as the leisure centres were open again I went back to training. On New Year's Eve I went out with my niece Sandra to see the New Year in. I wanted to be out doing something brilliant and having fun. We went to a club, where I did manage one drink, and we stayed at the club until 1.30 am. I had a really good night, although they didn't have enough R & B music, but I could live without that for one night.

I didn't make myself any promises or any New Year plans. I was just going to take one day at a time and look forward to better times. The eating plans were working alright, although it was hard to get back into eating properly during the Christmas holiday. I found it really hard to go shopping for myself. This was another thing that I really struggled with - going to the supermarket. I could only cope with buying one thing at a time like chicken, sandwiches, salad bowls, quiches or fish. I just tend to buy other items like rich tea biscuits and jelly babies. I buy sweet things to keep my sugar levels up and that is all I buy. I cannot buy more than one item, such as a quiche, which I will have for dinner. Then another time I will buy chicken and have that for dinner on its own. I really struggle to have any of these meals without feeling guilty and bad for eating them.

After the break, I had some good days when I was able to cope with meals, coming in early and having coffee and some toast. Then there were days I couldn't cope with it. I felt that it was all too much for my manager, who had taken on such a hard task in supporting me. She didn't know enough about eating disorders. Most people just think that someone with an eating disorder needs to eat and everything will be perfect in their world again; once they start to eat they are totally cured. If only that were true! My friends at work tried to help me too. They encouraged me and made suggestions, some of which were very difficult for me, i.e. eating in the staff room in front of half the staff team. There was no way I could cope with that. I could just about cope with eating in front of one person, never mind a room full of people. The progress I had made since coming out of hospital was steady but not consistent; but it was the most progress since my eating disorder began. Although managers and colleagues expected more from me, I did try really hard. I felt I had done well, trying to work towards changing my eating plan.

68. 2009: Struggles with eating at work

I now had to try and eat at work. I knew that this was going to be a struggle – it wasn't going to easy but I was going to give it a go. I had toast in the morning at work with a drink of coffee. At lunchtime I had whatever was on the menu, which could be cheese-and-potato pie with beans or chicken and vegetables. I really struggled with eating at work. I had a battle going on in my head saying that I was greedy and fat - I shouldn't be eating it ... I'd get fat - I just could not see past these thoughts. It felt like I was being tormented. In the end it was easier for me to stop eating at work. I couldn't get rid of these thoughts. But by stopping eating at work, I annoyed everyone and made them angry with me. I couldn't do it to make everyone happy, I had to do it for myself. I know my manager was supporting me by allowing me to eat in her office; it just didn't work, however, and it became a battle between me and them.

I need to be a bit stronger and I need to work through these thoughts. Maybe I'm not strong enough. By not eating during the day my work was affected, for I was often tired. I told myself that I didn't need to eat anything. I knew that I felt better, and was able to work better, when I had eaten and drunk something during the day, but it was the thoughts in my head that I couldn't cope with.

69. Losing my Friend

Early in April 2009 I arrived at work at 8:30am, to be asked by a member of staff if I had heard? I didn't have a clue what she meant by that. She then asked if she could have a word. I said yes, but was beginning to worry about what she was going to tell me. We both went into a room and sat down. I couldn't have prepared myself for what she was about to tell me. She told me that Rosie had died in a house fire. I was just so shocked. I asked, "When?" "How?" She continued to say that someone from work had had a phone call the previous evening. After I had been told, I just went to the nursery – I could see the look of shock and disbelief on everyone's faces. The feeling of unbelief stayed with me. People asked me if I was alright – what could I say? I thought about all the good times we'd had together - tennis lessons, laughs, days out – she had been a great friend. Her life had been cut short at 36 years old.

At the end of the day after we'd finished work, I went down to Rosie's house with Stacey and another colleague to put some flowers down. After that, I just needed to be on my own. The funeral was a very sad occasion but it was a very special one. Rosie had a beautiful send-off.

I still really struggle. I still feel I need to exercise every day. Because I eat, I feel I must go to the gym. I have made a lot of positive steps, but I know there is a lot more to be done.

70. Present Day

I have found it difficult to write this book; some of my feelings and thoughts I have kept very private and close to my heart. I haven't shared a lot of my feelings with my family or my close friends. I have found that writing my thoughts has been very therapeutic at times, and easier than seeing a therapist. When I see a therapist I struggle to explain myself. I struggle to open up in sessions, which is why I think therapy does not work very well with me.

I cannot give you a perfect end to this story. I would love to say that I am now better and have a normal relationship around food and exercise, but that would not be true. My body gets very tired easily and I get one infection after another, so my immune system is weak. I used to be able to exercise first thing in the morning, 7 a.m., everyday before I went to work. I now struggle with that, and can only go twice a week if my body will allow me to. I have become very frustrated and impatient with my recovery, because I always thought it would happen after treatment. I built myself up over the years and I still build myself up for failure, unfortunately.

I have received all these treatments and efforts to help me:

1) Day care treatment.
2) In-patients treatment.
3) Therapists who needed me to open up.
4) I also put my trust in prayer, hoping that was going to give me instant recovery.
5) Working with Cruse

It is not that these treatments have not worked, for they have helped me up to a point. I felt every time I went into hospital for treatment that it was chipping away at the emotional pain which was causing my eating disorder. Therapy was very hard most of the time; I struggled to talk about my emotions. I found I couldn't open up to my therapists and couldn't really trust them. I didn't feel they would understand me, so I kept them out. This made therapy difficult. I also haven't been able to deal with all the bereavements. I do not feel I will ever come to terms with my dad's death. I never grieved when my dad died, and because of all the other pressures I had afterwards, I guess I didn't have any time to deal with it properly.

A lot of my family and friends have been very supportive over the years, but I also feel they have put a lot of their faith in the hospital and treatments too. Any eating disorder stems from an emotional problem and I have discovered that somehow I must keep chipping away at these emotional problems.

Unless I deal with the pain and heartache of losing so many people I love and care about, I will find it hard to make a full recovery. I also feel there is a lot of pain and anger that I still have not really dealt with, so I cannot move on with my life. I also think it is very important for people to understand that because I look well it doesn't mean that there isn't a problem. People normally see an eating disorder as a slimming disease which you can just snap out of. You can go and have a meal and everything will be alright (if only it was as simple as that). But it is a bigger problem than just a slimming disease. Although my weight is not as low as 4 stone that doesn't mean that there is no problem. Just because my weight appears to be normal, it hides the fact that I have a very difficult disorder.

I've always wanted to write my true story, ending up with being well. I wanted a happy ending, but I have learnt through my journey with this disorder that you don't recover overnight. This is a very slow, difficult illness which is very hard to cure. There is no pill that will cure; hospital admission can't; therapy is not the answer. When I became ill I needed hospital treatment, and by working with professional support I have begun to slowly chip away at this illness. I know that I have to work at addressing my inner pain and discomforts. I have to accept I have an eating disorder, but I have made some progress:

1.   I am now able to drink with a group of people.
2.   I am sometimes able to eat with family and friends.
3.   I am able to eat out at restaurants (this used to be a no-no).
4.   There are no set times for me to eat.

I still have a long way to go. I struggle with completing meals. This always makes me feel greedy and bad, so I cannot finish a meal. I have no idea how to plan meals, and find it difficult to go shopping for myself. I tend to buy chicken on it's own - to me that is a meal. I still battle with exercise and find it hard to control it and keep to one class. This is because I still believe I am overweight and need to lose weight.

71. Treatment

I still see a therapist. I have now decided that I don't wish to continue to talk about my losses any more, for I feel that I need to move on. I am still an out-patient at the local hospital. I have now realised that no-one can fix anyone that has an eating disorder. The only one who can do this is me, with support. I have decided that I do not want to talk about my dad, mum and George because I feel that it is time to move on in my life, and while I am still thinking about them, I am living in the past. No amount of therapy is going to heal the pain and hurt of losing a loved one - time is the only thing that will help. I will never forget them, and they will always live on in my heart.

I also feel that friends and family are fed up with me. I guess it's because I keep talking about my disorder, and they don't see me trying to change (to them, change is eating three meals a day). They don't realise it's a lot more than that, and it's very much harder than that. I am taking one day at a time, and I will continue to make small steps to continue my recovery.

So, to all those out there who have this problem, or if you have family members or friends, just keep listening and never give up on them or yourself. Remember, small steps – it will not happen overnight.

At times I have not accepted that I have a problem because it is too difficult to deal with, and it is much easier to block it all out, not thinking about it at all. I know I have to deal with my low self-esteem, and my anger. I know that I have to find another best friend. I can't hold on to the illness and have it as my best friend. This illness will hurt me both emotionally and physically, because that is what disorders do. They can never be a best friend.

I have to go on battling my eating disorder. It is really hard, but I have to keep chipping away. At many times through all the treatment, I was fortunate to get support from other people. I find this very difficult because I find it very hard to let anyone in to help, which isn't helping with this illness. I just worry about my friends' and family's reaction to it all – whether they will just get angry and tell me to sort it out. I already get the usual comments that only I can sort it out - I think I know that by now! I think that this is the usual reaction to me or anyone that has this sort of problem. I am trying my best to sort myself out. I don't want to put any pressure on anyone else with my illness.

I think a lot about my dad, my brother George and my mum. I think about their strong faith in God. I always remember how strong my mum's faith was, and what a strong woman of God she was. That I will never forget - it amazed me. My mum went through a lot during her lifetime, but she never gave up on God. She kept her faith until the end of her life.

My dad was my hero. I think I have his sense of humour because I can come out with some stupid one-liners. George was so special, I loved the way he would work out every problem. I miss him so much, the way he would talk to me and guide me. I miss them all so much...they all took a part of me with them. They all taught me that if your mind keeps telling you that you can manage, the heart will also tell you not to give up. My dad, George and mum all told me to stand up and keep fighting, and in the end I hope things will be a lot easier.

Special mention to my nieces and nephews;

I love you all so much, and you have kept me going through the hard times. You all have been an inspiration. I love you all.

Alethea
I am so proud of you, you have always been very caring and I enjoy spending time with you.

Lisa
I am so proud of everything that you have done in your life. You are so intelligent. I really enjoy our chats.

Anton
I am proud; you really have grown up to be a bright, intelligent young man. I am so amazed when I spend time with you. You really inspire me.

Nadine
I am proud of you. My heart just melts when I hear you sing – your voice is amazing. I love spending time with you. Keep working hard, and I am sure your dreams will come true.

Kieran
I love you so much and I am proud of you. Keep working hard at School. I enjoy spending time with you.

Adena
I am so proud of you. Keep working hard and keep believing in yourself. I enjoy spending time with you.